What Next in Mission?

What Next in Mission?

by
PAUL A. HOPKINS

THE WESTMINSTER PRESS

Philadelphia

Scripture quotations from the Revised Standard Version of Bible are copyrighted 1946, 1952, © 1971,
1973 by the Division of Christian Education of the
National Council of the Churches of Christ in the
U.S.A., and are used by permission.

BOOK DESIGN BY DOROTHY ALDEN SMITH

First edition

Published by The Westminster Press®
Philadelphia, Pennsylvania

PRINTED IN THE UNITED STATES OF AMERICA

9 8 7 6 5 4 3 2 1

Library of Congress Cataloging in Publication Data

Hopkins, Paul A   1916–
    What next in mission?

    Includes bibliographical references.
    1. Mission of the church. I. Title.
BV601.8.H66   266   77–21776
ISBN 0–664–24143–3

Contents

Preface

While speaking with church groups around the country I have encountered their view of world mission. It generally reflects the idea that mission is primarily concerned with "our missionaries." When they hear a current statement of what the missionary situation is they respond, "Why haven't we been told these things before?"

This book was conceived as an answer to that question. The changing nature of mission has been widely covered in mission literature. The problem has been that most of this material has been directed to the professionals in the field. The laity is not generally well informed.

In this book I have attempted to communicate with the persons who support the mission of the church. While I am indebted to others for most of the positions taken herein, a few are my own and obviously subject to debate. This book is written for study in the church, and my intention is that it will help to further that discussion.

My hope also is that this study will contribute to the understanding that today we are engaged with Christians around the world in Christ's mission. When we fully grasp this fact we will be compelled to draw anew from the Scriptures the nature of our Lord's mission and the demands he is now making of us.

1

The Changing Mission
of the Church

The call for a moratorium, for many, seemed to end the missionary movement. "As a matter of policy, and as the most viable means of giving the African Church the power to perform its mission, . . . our option has to be *a moratorium* on the receiving of money and personnel." Thus spoke the Lusaka Assembly of the All-Africa Conference of Churches in 1974.[1] It was like the sound of a slamming door.

Recently, a woman who attended a mission conference listened intently to a plenary panel discussion at which moratorium became the main theme. Later at a workshop where the need for mission was being presented she shook her head in confusion. "What am I to believe? This morning I left the auditorium convinced that neither our money nor our missionaries are wanted. Now you are telling me that is not so." Her confusion is understandable; it is also widely shared.

Western churches are hearing divergent voices from their historic mission areas. Some voices call for a radical change in the forms of assistance; other voices cry, "Missionary, go home!" These same churches also face constituencies—supporting congregations—in which the understanding of mission is limited to the sending out of missionaries to do evangelistic work. Few church members understand the demands of overseas churches or grasp the impact of nationalism on the missionary movement. In attempting to respond to the needs of related churches abroad, mission boards and agencies lose the support of their constituencies at home.

"The depth of the crisis is indicated by the fact that the amount of money given for missionary work is decreasing in most large denominations," writes Jose Miguez-Bonino, president of Union Theological Seminary in Buenos Aires, Argentina. He goes on to say, "If it is not in others, it is because some churches are usually a few years late in being hit by the crisis."[2]

Churches and mission boards respond to this pressure by engaging in self-examination and reorganization. Generally the results show more insecurity than resolution. Perhaps that is why some overseas church leaders are even talking about overthrowing "the system." Burgess Carr, General Secretary of the All-Africa Conference of Churches, the regional ecumenical council, writes: "Mission Boards and missionary societies are perpetrators of structural violence at the deepest level of our humanity in the so-called Younger Churches, and they should be abolished."[3]

It seems obvious that a crisis of this dimension needs to be faced, not compromised. Mission agencies, which have tended to absorb the "heat" from overseas churches and constituencies at home, are crumbling under the task. A solution has not been found in reorganization. At the same time, many denominations are experiencing the birth of new mission initiatives committed to sending out the missionaries which the boards cannot or do not care to commission. Such competing efforts seem counterproductive to a denomination's witness in mission both at home and abroad. What are the issues? Are there alternatives, or is the mission era finished?

Some of the Issues

Almost fifteen years ago a leader of the Coptic Evangelical Church of Egypt put it this way: "We would like to go to heaven with the help of brothers. But if you want to send us to heaven by being our masters, we prefer to go to hell." That quotation is more instructive if one tries to sense the emotional content rather than understand the symbolism.

The age of nationalism in which we live did not create the resentment of subject people to those who colonized them. Rather, the resentment created nationalism. The tragic fact is that far too many missionaries have fallen victim to a sense of their own superiority. The harvest they have reaped is the resentment now being expressed. And at the heart of Western superiority lie racial attitudes. Few missionaries would admit to the guilt of racism. The people of darker skin to whom they minister are, however, almost unanimous in condemning the missionary community in this regard.

In part, both of the above grow out of another issue: Western economic advantage. Quite recently a leader of one African church raised the question: "Why is it that a missionary pastor of one of our churches is paid three times what his African colleague receives even though both have equal responsibilities? Each buys the same food, pays the same amount for rent, has the same transportation costs, and has equal costs for the schooling of children. What is the justification for such discrimination except that the missionary is paid by his church in the West and the African is paid by his congregation?"[4] The question then is why should not all salaries, missionary and national, be pooled and each receive the same.

Or consider the question, Whom does the missionary serve? It has been raised with increasing frequency for many years, but no unequivocal answer has been forthcoming from the so-called sending churches. Spiritually speaking, the missionary is in God's service. But on the day-to-day level, does the missionary work for the church that pays the missionary's salary or for the overseas church that has called the missionary? Most mission agencies have a policy statement to the effect that missionaries are subject to the church to which they are sent. In practice, however, that policy seldom works. Decisions regarding salary, furloughs, education of children, ownership of an automobile, and even some factors involving the work to which they are assigned, are matters within the province of the missionary and the sending church. Often, however, decisions in these areas have serious impact upon the witness and life of the church to which the missionary is assigned.

Also, as America in particular has fallen under the pervasive influence of the affluent society, the spiritual deterioration of the church in the United States has come into question. Such matters as easy divorce and remarriage, uninhibited sexual life-styles, corruption in business, Watergate, decline in church membership—all these and other matters are viewed with deep concern in churches overseas. Now, the problems mentioned previously are seen, not as warts on an otherwise healthy church, but as expressions of a debilitated spiritual life. One African friend, reflecting on all of this, said: "My point is that America needs to take her missionaries unto herself for a while and reflect on her shortcomings, leaving us free to deal with ours."[5]

Why Mission Agencies Don't Act

If all these issues have been known to mission agencies, why haven't they done something about them? Why have the mission agencies waited for calls for moratorium? The answer has already been suggested: Rightly or wrongly, the mission agencies feel caught in the middle. They do relate to overseas churches from which these expressions arise. At the same time, most church members at home continue to think of mission in terms of missionaries who preach Christ to the heathen. They are either unaware or forgetful that through the nineteenth-century missionary movement the church of Jesus Christ has been extended to almost every nation on earth. All churches are under mandate to tell others about the good news of Jesus the Christ. Recently, research has spread the word that these churches in what is called the Third World—the world beyond the Western countries and the Marxist countries of Eastern Europe—are growing faster than churches in America.

Briefly stated, that is the nature of the crisis. Before we go on to look at these issues in greater depth and seek to discern the future, a brief review of the history of the church in mission may be helpful to our quest for understanding.

"You Shall Be My Witnesses"

The church of Jesus Christ has been, from its beginning, a community of people who are interested in others. From the time of our Lord's command to his followers to be his witnesses, the church has used the available means of communication and routes of trade to tell the good news of the Kingdom of God. These efforts which have been most effective in the planting of new communities of believers have come to be known as missionary movements.

The first of these is recorded in the book of Acts. It tells how the early apostles moved through the Roman Empire to spread the news about the resurrected Lord. Others who had come to know the story of what had happened in Jerusalem and who had become followers of Christ were also bearers of the news. Visitors coming from far places heard rumors of the story and sought for confirmation. The whole region was alive with the news about the life, death, and resurrection of Jesus the Christ. Those who believed formed fellowships that offered love and meaning to those who joined them. The quality of their life together stood in sharp contrast to the vulgar and brutal society of that day. The story of Christ was indeed good news!

The new faith soon became noticed by the politician priests of the Roman Empire and persecution fell upon the newly formed Christian communities. A new God was no threat to the polytheism of the Empire, but a new sect that refused to acknowledge the emperor as God was something else. Soon those who refused allegiance to the emperor by verbal confession that "Caesar is Lord" were to learn of Caesar's power to harm and punish. So the book of Acts tells us that the believers "were scattered because of the persecution" (Acts 11:19), and wherever the Christians went, the church took root and grew. Thus it was that Tertullian in the second century said to the Roman persecutors: "The more ye mow us down, the more we grow, the seed is the blood of Christians."[6] And so it was that Christians who could not be silent about the good news of Jesus Christ—even at peril of life—carried the gospel story across the Roman Empire.

The Conquest of the Roman Empire

Church history suggests that there were probably ten major persecutions under the Roman Caesars. The first serious persecution, and probably the most widely known, was under Nero about A.D. 64. Tradition tells us that both Peter and Paul suffered martyrdom under Nero. Succeeding persecutions were at times even more violent than that of Nero's rule. Through them all, the Christians suffered, died, and were driven from their homes. But always they told the story of Jesus Christ, their Lord, who had brought the good news of the Kingdom of God. And through all the persecutions the number of Christian communities grew, even to the point of penetrating Caesar's household. In at least the case of Emperor Diocletian, his wife and daughter embraced the Christian faith.[7]

Under such circumstances it would be highly unusual had everyone who named Christ as Lord remained faithful. Some faced torture fearlessly and others fled. Some recanted, others wavered and tried to find ways both to save their lives and hold their faith. In the end, however, it was the witness of the faithful which caused

some of the regional Caesars to revolt against the persecution edicts. In some areas the anti-Christian measures
were allowed to lapse. Finally, with the crowning of
Constantine as emperor in A.D. 323, the Christian
church was officially recognized; the Christian faith had
conquered the Empire.

Ebb and Flow

Our purpose is not to provide a definitive history of
the church in mission, but to catch something of what
Latourette refers to as its "ebb and flow." We have just
noted the phenomenal growth of the Christian church
under persecution until the time of its acceptance
under Constantine. But success has often proved to be
the setting for recession.

Having received the favor of the emperor, Christians
soon came into positions of power in the Empire. In
return, the emperor gained power in the church. This
proved to be a mixed blessing. It has been said that
Christianity both weakened and prolonged the Roman
Empire and Greco-Roman culture.

The Christian faith quickly spread throughout the
Empire after Constantine's conversion to the faith;
later it began to penetrate pagan areas beyond the Empire. However, another factor was at work. Latourette
writes: "That Christianity was seriously affected by the
fatal sickness of the Roman Empire is one of the most
palpable facts of history. For more than four centuries
the outcome was by no means clear. In the numbers of
those who called themselves Christian, in apparent
inner vitality as expressed in fresh movements inspired
by the faith, in the moral and spiritual quality of the
churches which were the official vehicles of the Gospel,

and in its prominence in the total human scene, Christianity lost ground."[8] The Christian church had become infected with the virus of national religion: Success brought privilege and power; it also brought corruption and confusion. The problems that followed are those which continue to plague the church and its mission until today.

The fall of Rome and the sweep of Islam across Africa and into Europe resulted in a period of recession for Christianity roughly between the years A.D. 500 and 950. Then a new movement began. Latourette says: "The century which was bounded by A.D. 950 and A.D. 1050 saw as wide a geographic advance of Christianity as any in the history of the faith until after A.D. 1500. It witnessed the conversion of those pagans who so recently had been a scourge of Christendom, the Scandinavians, in some of their homelands—Denmark, Norway, and, incompletely, in Sweden—and in lands beyond the earlier borders of 'Christendom' in which they had effected settlements—Iceland, Greenland, and, more notably, Kiev, the nucleus of the later Russia."[9]

This movement was to continue beyond its main surge until about 1350. In contrast to other movements that had followed military conquest, the Scandinavian outreach had been the result of the conquerors' contact with the Christians of England.

Another period of recession followed, from about 1350 to 1500. In the East the Ottoman Turks had established their power and severely repressed many of the Orthodox churches. Only the Russian Orthodox Church grew in strength during this period.

In the West the Russian Church suffered from schism and internal struggles, while the spiritual state of the papacy, monastic life, and political life reflected the decay of this period. It was a time of the breaking down of the social order. Whether the church suffered from the same disease as the social fabric in general or whether the social fabric suffered because of the faith-lessness of the church is a question not answered by the historians.

The period between 1500 and 1750 was one of a significant outward movement of Christianity. It was largely the result of the Spanish and Portuguese explo-ration. Roman Catholic missions sprang up wherever these explorers made discoveries of new lands and new peoples. This was also the period of the Protestant Ref-ormation and of the Counter-Reformation in the Roman Church. This latter event gave considerable missionary zeal to the then great colonial powers—Spain and Portugal. The Protestant movement was too busy consolidating its freedom from Rome and develop-ing its theology to have a deep concern for missionary activity. The Protestant missionary movement came later, following the Evangelical revival, which in turn had followed the brief recession in Christianity that began about 1750. That recession was related to the so-called Age of Reason which was popular throughout western Europe. "Man, so it was held, had heretofore been bound by ignorance and superstition. Now, by the use of reason he was achieving emancipation and there was nothing that, with this tool, he could not hope to accomplish."[10]

The Evangelical Revival

The nineteenth-century missionary movement had its roots in the Evangelical revival. For that reason we need to look a bit more closely at this period. The latest ebb in the growth of the church followed the scientific discoveries of the Age of Reason. The mood of Europe was such that educated people had little time for the church. Some thinkers were challenging the truths of Christianity. Literature and art were more concerned with secular subjects and less devoted to specifically Christian themes. "Western Europe," Latourette tells us, "was outgrowing the faith which had done much to guide and shape its infancy and that what survived of that faith was being perverted to man's hurt and was destroying such remnants of itself as persisted."[11]

J. Wesley Bready, who chronicles the time in a more intimate manner, speaks of how men, women, and children were hanged for some 160 violations of law. "Throughout most of the century, in cities and on highways, were to be seen gallows, often with their last corpses 'left rotting in chains'—a gruesome warning to the populace. . . . Not infrequently seven, ten or fifteen culprits were executed at the same time and place, and these occasions came to be styled 'Hanging Shows.' "[12]

Bready goes on: "The rule of law had broken down; constables often passed by a notorious robber, not daring to apprehend him lest a gang of armed villains rush to his assistance. As late as 1751, Horace Walpole, writing to Sir Horace Mann, complains: 'One is forced to travel, even at noon, as if one were going to battle.' "[13]

It was at this point in the tearing of Europe's social fabric that Britain began to hear the preaching of John Wesley. Wesley, a priest in the Church of England, had been influenced by the nonconformist movement. After considerable restlessness and travel, while listening to the reading of Luther's preface to the epistle to the Romans, he records in his journal: "I felt my heart strangely warmed. I felt I did trust in Christ, Christ alone for salvation: and an assurance was given me that he had taken away my sins, even mine, and saved me from the law of sin and death."[14] Thus Wesley's life and preaching were transformed and the Methodist movement was begun.

Latourette, attempting to explain the popularity of Wesley's preaching in these times, says: "In spite of widespread vulgarity, drunkenness, obscenity, and calloused cruelty in eighteenth century Britain, and a large degree of religious illiteracy and scepticism, there was a general, even if superficial knowledge of the main tenets of Christian teaching about morals and faith. In many, although a minority, there was a hunger left unsatisfied by the formal services in most of the churches."[15]

And so, in Britain was born the Evangelical Awakening. "In the opinion of many historians, it saved England from a social revolution."[16] The social impact of the revival under Wesley resulted in prison reform, schools for the previously neglected miners, regulations regarding child labor, the abolition of the slave trade in the British Empire, and the establishment of Sierra Leone as a refuge for freed slaves. But more revelant to this study was the beginning of what is popularly called the nineteenth-century missionary movement.

The Nineteenth-Century Missionary Movement

In 1792 the Baptist Missionary Society was organized, primarily as a result of the work of William Carey, a self-educated teacher, shoemaker, and pastor. Later came the London Missionary Society, and soon after that came what today is called the Church Missionary

Society of the Church of England. Within the last decade of the eighteenth century a group of men and women who had been transformed by the Evangelical Awakening knew that its impact could not be contained within the British Isles. In response to the New Testament command to "preach the gospel to every creature" the modern missionary movement was launched.

At this time, the church of Jesus Christ found expression essentially, although not entirely, in three major traditions: Eastern Orthodoxy, Protestantism, and Roman Catholicism. The latter prevailed widely in western Europe, dominated as it was by its Roman roots. It had, however, through the period of Spanish and Portuguese world domination, put forth outposts in Latin America, Africa, and parts of Asia. On the whole, these were limited establishments, mostly trading posts and mission stations where the Iberian conquerors had established military control. Yet this outreach by the Roman Church was significant for the Christian church. The movement launched as a result of the Evangelical Awakening in Britain was in some ways its Protestant counterpart. However, the impact of the persistent outreach was not only to revitalize the totality of the Christian church but also to make it truly a worldwide body.

The vitality of this movement has been demonstrated by its longevity. Through wars, depressions, and great political upheavals this movement has continued to carry out an effective witness to Jesus Christ. As the nineteenth century drew to a close a great forward surge came through the formation of the Student Volunteer Movement for Foreign Missions which took as its watchword "The evangelization of the world in this generation."[17] The statistical record suggests that by 1900 there were more than 450 million throughout the world who called themselves Christians.

In the period of the missionary century, Christianity had outstripped every other religion in the number of its professed adherents. More important was the tremendous influence that Christianity had upon all mankind. Wherever its impact was felt, a new social consciousness arose which brought not only social reform but in many places economic development as well. Latourette has given us an excellent summary of the advance of Christian faith in this period: "More than any other religion in human history it was becoming universal. Its history had demonstrated that it appealed to individuals in all races, nations, and stages of culture and that among those who accepted it specific fruits appeared which were clearly recognizable. Each major forward wave had carried the faith into additional portions of the earth's surface. Each recession had been less marked than its predecessor. In the advances of the post-A.D. 1500 periods Christianity had become worldwide to an extent attained by no other religion. Especially after A.D. 1815 it had been planted among practically all peoples and tribes and after A.D. 1914 was becoming firmly rooted in the texture of their cultures."[18]

Truly the nineteenth-century missionary movement had been tremendously successful in planting the church of Jesus Christ throughout the world. The cost in lives of those who died of tropical diseases and were buried where they labored, and the fortune which members of churches at home gave to support this great movement, can never be fully comprehended. Nor was anyone asking for an accounting. Those who labored to accomplish this great task had done so because they followed their Lord's command, "Go. . . ."

Those who gave saw results far more impressive than any accountant's statement. The church of Jesus Christ is a reality throughout the entire globe.

QUESTIONS FOR DISCUSSION

1. This chapter suggests something of a revolution against the missionary sending agencies. In what respects are the feelings of Third World churches justified? In what lands that used to be called "mission fields" are the churches rapidly growing? If these churches are growing faster than ours in the United States, why do we still hear so much about the need to send evangelistic missionaries from America to these nations?

2. The section "You Shall Be My Witnesses" expresses something of how the gospel was truly good news to those who heard it in the first century. In what way is the gospel good news in your community? How does that differ, if at all, from how the gospel is understood by those who hear it in an African or Asian community?

3. What are the "pervasive influences of the affluent society" in the United States? How do the pressures that these influences bring to bear on today's church differ from the persecutions experienced under the Roman Caesars?

4. In what way does the nineteenth-century missionary movement differ from the earlier period of the expansion of the church? In view of this history of ebb and flow in the expansion of the church throughout the world, what evidence can you cite to indicate that the nineteenth-century missionary movement

has been completed? Are we living in an "ebb" period?

5. In speaking of the Age of Reason, Latourette suggests that there was nothing that human beings felt incapable of achieving through the use of reason. In what ways does that view prevail today? What is its effect upon missionary outreach? How is our social context similar to that described in England prior to the Evangelical Awakening?

2

How We Got Where We Are

In the nineteenth century the missionary was a central figure in the life of the church. There was good reason for this emphasis. God used the missionary to reach out to areas of the world where Christ's name was not known. It was through the missionary that many peoples in all parts of the earth first heard the gospel. From the time of Paul until the modern missionary movement, the missionary was the spearhead of advance of the Christian faith.

The missionary has not sought personal prestige or privilege, but has sought the proclamation of the gospel and the formation of the church. The missionary's relationship to the church should be a shining example of what John the Baptist said about his relationship to Christ: "He must increase, but I must decrease" (John 3:30).

The Missionary and the Supporting Churches

That simile suggests a part of the problem. It is well illustrated in a book about mission work in China. The writer states: "A good many missionary-minded people at home are more interested in the conquests of the

gospel than they are in the building up of the indigenous church. Missionaries, when they come home on
furlough, are expected to tell thrilling stories of spectac-
ular conversions among the heathen: emaciated opium
sots smashing their poisonous pipes into a thousand
pieces; inveterate gamblers delivered overnight from
the grip of China's greatest vice; head-hunters tamed
by the power of the cross. . . . Such stories make good
messages! Such men must be good missionaries!"[19]

The problem between the missionary and the supporting church at home, in part at least, grows out of the
motivation of those who support the cause of mission.
As noted above, the missionary who has good stories to
tell of God's work among the heathen is likely to be
considered a good missionary and to be well supported.
One who gets a native church going so that it can thrive
on its own may be regarded as a failure.

Mission boards that send out missionaries of the first
kind also get support. For that reason they have done
too little to establish a Scriptural motivation for mission
among supporting congregations. To this day, support
tends to follow "success stories." A cursory study of
missionary interpretation materials suggests that mission agencies have continued to use missionary success
stories to raise funds for the work of missions. They have
failed to interpret the changing character of mission so
that it is understood and supported.

This failure has contributed to the rise of what has
been called the "missionary empire." It is interesting to
note the difference between a mission executive's description of this problem and the description of an overseas church leader. The mission executive writes: "During the lush era of nineteenth-century Western
imperialism and its influence on the development of

the 'mission compound' mentality, some missionaries built their empires and justified them by the accepted standards of their day."[20]

Contrast that description with the emotion contained in the following: "Those individuals who were being sent out . . . were to become powerful money-raisers, so powerful that the church which sent them would eventually lose control over them. I know of several instances where the 'missionary,' as he was called, has become a problem for the denomination. He turned out to be such a good fund raiser that the denomination became afraid that it had to go along with him, or else he would raise his own funds, return to the land of the 'native' and do his own thing independently."[21]

Some of the terms in the above quotations may need to be explained. A mission compound is a complex of mission buildings on land that a mission may have received by grant from the ruling authority to develop for its work. It may or may not be fenced or walled about. That is essentially irrelevant. Within the compound there may be a hospital, a school, and missionary housing. Frequently, but not always, there would be housing for local employees. The expression "mission compound mentality" refers to the manner in which missionaries who lived in the compounds tended to think. During the day he or she would be in full charge of a given activity—that is, school, hospital, etc. Orders would be given to national employees as though they were servants. Only infrequently would there be an opportunity to talk over implications of such orders or the reasons from which they arose. Usually the local employee had little or no knowledge of the purpose of the work, because "mission policy discussions" were

limited only to missionary personnel on the mission station or compound.

At night the missionaries would retire into their
homes. Their local employees would have cleaned the
house and prepared the meals. The missionary family
would be served during the meals by the local person,
who would also wash the dishes, clear the kitchen, and
then disappear until the morning when quite early he
(house "servants" almost always are!) would be back to
prepare breakfast and begin another day's work.

The use of servants was justified in a number of ways.
Primarily it gave the foreign missionaries more freedom to be about the work to which they had been
called. It was also justified as a means of providing employment for local people. Each of these points could
have been valid. The problem arises in matters of relationship. Why should the person who performs these
services be treated like a servant? Either such a person
is a brother or sister in Christ or a person to whom the
missionary should be a witness of Christ's love. The
servant-master relationship simply cannot be justified
in either case.

The problem of fair wages for national employees is
both important and complicated. Many local people
may also have servants. For the missionary to pay the
same wages that local people pay would appear to be
exploitation by the rich foreigner. To pay more than the
prevailing wage would create problems in what is likely
to be the rural setting of the compound. The missionary
should always have lived with these issues in tension;
they are not totally resolvable. Too often they were not
given a second thought.

Out of such an environment grew the tendency on
the part of even some of the better missionaries to "talk

down" to those to whom they came to witness of God's love. The mission compound mentality has produced many of the "radical" church leaders in the indigenous churches of our day. It also has produced the type of nationals who will say what they think the foreigner wants to hear. The latter are dehumanized people who are despised by their own community; the former are among those who today speak harshly against the missionary.

But what has been described so far is the normal mission compound. At times there have been the gifted fund raisers who "built their own empires." Such persons may be doctors who almost single-handedly raise the funds to build hospitals. Some may even be evangelists whose fund-raising ability makes it possible for them to control a whole compound such as described above. Good work may have been accomplished by such people, but almost inevitably the power involved in controlling so much money causes problems of relationship between nationals and missionaries, and among the missionaries with whom the empire builder works. And as indicated above, the denominational agency responsible for the work is unable to resolve such issues because the gifted fund raiser has more access to the supporting churches at home than do denominational executives.

Such factors affect congregational giving in support of mission and make decisions about the distribution of mission income more difficult. Too often there is a tendency to form attachments. "Dr. X is such a godly person and so successful as a missionary; we always ask him to our missionary conferences and our people support his work heavily." Questions about the work that is thus supported are seldom raised. No effort is made to deter-

mine how Dr. X may be viewed by the people he sup-
posedly is trying to win to Christ: These and other issues
are never seriously considered. Decisions are made on
the basis of charisma, and money tends to follow the
personality. The counterproductive nature of such individual or congregational giving is at the root of many of
today's mission problems.

The Missionary and the Indigenous Church

One of the most instructive conversations I have experienced on the subject of missionary–indigenous
church relationships was with a Ugandan refugee in
Juba, Sudan. It was after nightfall in that humid, heavy
atmosphere which is so common to the southern Sudan.
I was sitting outside the hotel talking with a friend
when Peter Ebe walked up and spoke to us. We soon
fell into serious conversation. I learned that Peter had
been a district commissioner in Uganda and had gotten
into trouble with the then current president of the
country. He was obviously a well-informed man and I
enjoyed listening to him expound on the various questions I posed.

Suddenly he stopped and said: "I've been answering
a lot of your questions and I don't know who you are.
What are you doing in Juba?" I explained that I worked
for the church and was involved in my church's mission
in Africa. That brought a strong expression of disgust
from my new friend: "I've got no time for the church.
I've had my fill of missionaries," he said. I urged him to
tell me why he felt as he did and a long story ensued.

The first missionaries that arrived in his part of
Uganda were wonderful people. They lived in the village and worked hard to learn the language. They told

the story about the good news of Jesus Christ and
proved their concern by showing his grandparents better farming methods and better hygiene. They also
helped to reduce the language of the people to writing
while teaching them to read and write. "My grandparents and the missionaries in those days were part of one
community. We accepted them and they accepted us.
We helped one another and contributed one to another. They were truly people of God."

As the story unfolded he told of the next generation
of missionaries. They came with increased Western support. They built Western-style houses because the
houses of his people were not good enough for them.
They brought furniture and other Western conve-
niences with them. But more important, they did not
live with the people. "They didn't have to," Peter said,
"because they learned our language from the first generation of missionaries and didn't need us like the old-
timers needed us."

When he got around to talking about the third generation of missionaries, those he grew up with, he couldn't
contain his disgust. They not only brought more and
more Western goods and lived culturally and socially
farther from the people, they actually showed their dis-
taste for the way the people lived and openly spoke of
the need for cultural change. Their superiority and arrogance was apparently so great that I could sense the
emotion rising in my new friend as he told the story. He
spoke of how they built large churches for the people,
and added that the churches were almost empty now.
The people would not return to those churches so long
as that kind of missionary remained in control. "Some-
day I hope that the people who have been trained by
this third generation of missionaries will rise up and

throw them out. Maybe then the kind of spirit which the first missionaries had will come to our people. If that should happen, the churches will again be filled."

About the time that the second generation of missionaries were at work in the area where Peter Ebe's father lived, a young missionary by the name of Roland Allen served for eight years in China. He was so concerned over what he had experienced that he returned to Britain, took a parish, and for some forty years gave his attention to studying and writing about missionary methods. One of his best-known works is entitled *Missionary Methods: St. Paul's or Ours?* Some of his insights are helpful in complementing what Mr. Ebe had to say:

"We have preached the Gospel from the point of view of the wealthy man who casts a mite into the lap of a beggar, rather than from the point of view of the husbandman who casts his seed into the earth, knowing that his own life and the lives of all connected with him depend upon the crop which will result from his labour. ... We have done everything for them except acknowledge any equality. ... We have treated them as 'dear children,' but not as 'brethren.'

"The moment it is suggested that a council in which natives are in a majority should have the power to direct the action of a white missionary, the moment it is suggested that a native, even though he may be a man of the highest devotion and intellectual ability, should be put into a position of authority in a province where white men still hold office, the white missionaries revolt.

"In everything we have taught our converts to turn to us, to accept our guidance. We have asked nothing from them but obedience.

"This is why we are so anxious to import the law and customs. This is why we set up constitutions containing all sorts of elaborate precautions against possible mistakes. We sometimes hope to educate the native in self-government by establishing councils, or synods, on which they are represented, but we hasten to take every possible precaution to avoid the possibility of their making any mistake or taking any action, even in the smallest matters of ritual or practice, which may be contrary to our ideas of what is proper.

"Moreover, the systems which we import are systems which we acknowledge to be full of imperfections, the sources of many difficulties and dangers at home. We bind on the new converts a burden heavy and grievous to be borne, a burden which neither we nor our fathers were able to bear; and we bind it upon a people who have not inherited it."[22]

The Mission Agencies: Part of the Problem

If ideas such as these arose some fifty years ago, why were they not adopted and made a part of the missionary movement at that time? In part, the answer lies in the spirit of the age, and in part, it was due to a great theological controversy which shook the American churches, including the missionary movement.

It was the time when World War I had made the world "safe for democracy." A growing spirit of liberalism in the church questioned the validity of the missionary enterprise and called for a greater tolerance of other religious traditions.

Latourette points out that in some parts of the Protestant Church "there was a feeling that all religions, including Christianity, arose from man's search for truth, that each had in it elements of truth, and that all had in them something of error."[23] This view was forth-rightly rejected by others, and in this way, as well as in other ways, the cause of mission became caught up in the liberal-conservative controversy of that period.

Much has been written about this time of great controversy in the church in America. It is the period that saw publication of a report by the Commission of Appraisal of the Laymen's Missionary Movement entitled *Re-thinking Missions*. This report became the epicenter of the liberal-conservative controversy in the field of missions. The section of the report termed "General Principles" took an appreciative attitude toward other faiths, which to many mission leaders seemed to destroy the motive for the missionary enterprise.

The International Missionary Council requested Hendrik Kraemer to write a volume in preparation for its Madras meeting in 1938 to counteract the inclusiveness expressed in the Laymen's report. Kraemer's book, *The Christian Message in a Non-Christian World,* and various articles, argued the case for the traditional principles of the missionary movement—that Christianity originated in the self-revelation of God in Christ and the other religions were the outgrowth of sinful man's beclouded groping for God.

This period also saw the rise of fundamentalism, the splintering of denominations, and the formation of many new Bible churches and faith missions. It was a turbulent time. Issues tended to center almost exclusively on whether a person belonged to the fundamentalist faction or to the "modernist" camp—a term applied to liberals.

The question of the true purpose of missions and the right policies to achieve that purpose was lost in the controversy. The valid points in the Commission of Appraisal's report were also lost in the larger quarrel about the exclusiveness of the Christian faith.

At this point the mission agencies became part of the problem instead of working for a solution. Support for the overseas mission had largely come from the conservative wing of the church. Instead of moving forward by adopting the obvious reforms that were needed while holding to the central thrust of the gospel message, the agencies tended to maintain the *status quo*. To hold the support of the conservatives, a policy of reinforcing the basic stance of the mission body in each area was pursued. While never a stated policy, this tacit agreement avoided controversy with the missionary power on the field, maintained constituency support, and generally precluded the raising of questions of basic policy reform at least at that time.

Essentially the missionary enterprise was reinforcing the observation of Roland Allen: "Long experience of difficulties, dangers, heresies, parties, schisms, has made us overcautious and has undermined our faith in the power of the Holy Ghost."[24] Thus, reform in the missionary movement was set back. Reaction to theological struggles in the home church seriously hindered the life and development of the younger churches. In many areas the result was to reinforce a relationship of dependence—the exact opposite of what Roland Allen had pleaded for in his writings.

Mission interpretation to the church at home was also inhibited by this theological struggle. The younger churches had been asking for more authority and responsibility in their own life. Presumably mission executives saw the inevitability of these demands. However, they did not share them with the supporting constituency until many years later. They feared that those who supported the mission of the church would feel that the agencies were irresponsible and might allow liberal ideas to creep into the minds of the leaders of the younger churches.

The Mission Agencies: Post-World War II

The period after World War II was a difficult one for the cause of missions. The long years from 1939 to 1945 caused the attrition of many career missionaries and there were few or no new appointments. With the coming of peace there was a period of resurgence. About the same time, the new nationalism of the Third World began to exert itself. Demands for political independence were soon echoed by church leaders seeking the end of Western missionary domination.

At that time, many overseas church bodies were organically tied to American church judicatories. This relationship was called into question as foreign domination. The mission bodies abroad were locally registered as foreign organizations and they had their own constitution and bylaws. This arrangement also came under fire. The newly independent churches were asking that these mission bodies be integrated into the new church.

But about the same time, the mission agencies received a financial shot in the arm. During what has come to be known as the "fabulous fifties," church membership and attendance reached new highs. So did church income for all causes, including mission work.

While this was happening, Latourette tells us, the younger churches were "coming of age" and had become sensitive to the domination of white missionaries.[25] Instead of assisting them in the development of their chosen leadership, the agencies sent a new flood of missionaries out into a world that was just beginning to taste revolution against Western power. The number of missionaries peaked about 1958, but the flow of money available for missionary work did not peak until the mid-sixties.

Perhaps it is possible to excuse those responsible in the mission agencies for this new flow of missionaries in the 1950's. They did not see as clearly then as we can now what God was doing. The success of mission work had been measured by the number of missionaries sent out by each agency, and in the postwar decade as money became available it was used in the customary way.

But as the picture became clearer, as the movement toward independence for the churches in the new nations became a flood, the situation demanded prompt action. At just this point the mission agencies exhibited a lack of "surefootedness" as they began to work in new and tense relationships.

It was not easy to bring missionaries home who had developed the kind of supporting constituency that would establish them despite agency action. A four-sided tension was beginning to develop: there was the "old style" missionary who had built a power base both at home and overseas; the national church in whose area the missionary worked; the mission agency; and the supporting constituency. Mission agency executives handled the matter in such a way as either to lose the confidence of the supporting churches or to give over control to them. Both of these courses of action boded ill for the future of the churches' mission.

This was the moment for dialogue with national

church leaders to seek solutions to the problems of the mission compounds, to ask which missionaries should continue to serve and which ones should be reassigned. But, once again, mostly because of concern for supporting constituencies, the matter was compromised. Missionaries who tendered resignations found them readily accepted. But missionaries who had powerful supporting constituencies at home were permitted to continue to serve abroad. Almost invariably they were the ones who gave the newly independent churches the most serious difficulties.

Perhaps the most significant cause of mission agency failure was a subtle one. We have noted that while the flow of missionaries peaked about 1958, the flow of support did not peak until the mid-sixties. This meant that the mission agencies had an increase of uncommitted funds. Some of these funds went to increased costs of missionary maintenance. It was a time when the standard of living in the United States was rising, and on the whole, missionary costs tended to keep pace with costs at home. But that was only one element. Another way in which these uncommitted funds were used was in "innovative programming" conceived and directed by the agencies. Some of these programs were of high priority to related churches abroad; others were of high priority only to the mission agency. In order to administer these new programs, agency staffs were increased. That was the third way in which uncommitted funds were used.

The psychological factor at work in all of this was that power began to move from the missionaries on the field to agency offices at home. In the earlier days of mission it would take the fastest ships months to carry mail to the agency and back to the missionary on the field. It was therefore essential that the missionaries be able to make most decisions on their own. Agency staffs tended to be small, working mainly with the supporting constituencies.

The power shift from the mission bodies overseas to the agency at home was brought about by a number of developments. Probably the most significant was the coming of rapid communications, particularly air mail. Nationalism was another factor that put the missionary on the defensive. Still another was the ability of the agencies to increase their grants to national churches in view of the increase they were experiencing in uncommitted funds.

Intuitively the missionary understood this and tension developed between the missionaries and the agency executives. What previously had been a close working relationship in a fellowship of spreading the gospel became a power struggle which eventually flowed over to the supporting churches.

For a while, the power of the agency was tolerated by the related church. The flow of missionaries had been cut down. Some of the priority programs of the related church were being funded by the agency. For these reasons the new church-agency relationship was tolerable. But that period was short-lived. The agency bureaucracy put increasing administrative burdens on overseas churches, burdens that these churches were unable to bear because of their lack of staff and funds. The very fact that power had flowed into the agency hands soon made it apparent that the mission agency itself was the problem.

It was inevitable that tensions would develop between the missionary and his supporting constituency, the overseas church, and the mission agency. The tension did not reach the breaking point until after the mid-sixties. By that time the supporting constituency was gaining the impression that the agencies had lost their vision for mission. Missionary interpretation had proved to be more effective than agency interpretation —and no one was really speaking on behalf of the church overseas. The failure of the agencies to give strong direction boded ill for the future of the missionary movement.

QUESTIONS FOR DISCUSSION

1. Considering the overseas mission program of your church, what priority would you give to the national church? What should be the goal of missionaries in regard to the strengthening of the church in which they work? How would you evaluate the overseas mission program to which you contribute?

2. As you read the story of Peter Ebe, think of "third generation" missionaries as being supported by your church. How would you be able to get the Ugandan view of such missionaries? How would those missionaries have understood the issue that Peter Ebe described? How would they present their work to your church while they are home on furlough?

3. What do the quotes from Roland Allen suggest to you regarding the attempt to keep overseas churches faithful to the traditions of your church in America? Why should there be the same denominational labels in overseas countries as in America? What reasons can you give for your denominational mission agency to support mission work outside your confessional fellowship?

4. Think of the most powerful mission interpretation you can remember. Were you most impressed by the material, the way the material was presented, or the personality of the speaker? What kind of mission interpretation information does your congregation need to make wise decisions regarding the distribution of mission funds?

5. When did your congregation have overseas church leaders speak on behalf of the priorities and goals of their churches?

3

God Is at Work Through the Church

Growth of Churches in the Third World

The extraordinary growth of the church in the so-called "mission fields" is a hidden miracle. It is hidden, of course, only to those who have not traveled through those countries or who have not heard or understood what God is doing.

Latourette points out that the percentage of Christians among non-Occidental peoples had approximately doubled between 1914 and 1944. "In some regions, notably in equatorial Africa, it had more than doubled."[26]

Ralph Winter, in his summary *The World Christian Movement 1950–1975,* points out that "the net increase in the number of Christians in the non-Western world by the end of this period (1975) was far larger than the total number of Christians in the non-Western world at the beginning of the period (1950). That is to say, in the non-Western world, Christians increased by 140 percent, while the general population increased by only 42 percent."[27]

David B. Barrett, director of the Unit of Research, Church of the Province of Kenya (Anglican), has made

some striking predictions: By the year A.D. 2000 there
will be 350 million Christians in Africa, 575 million in
Latin America, and 165 million in Asia. Together they
will number more than the total number of Christians
in Europe and North America.[28] If that prediction is
fulfilled, the center of the Christian world, numerically
speaking, will have shifted from its historic base in
Europe and North America to the areas of the former
missions.

This tremendous growth in the churches of the Third
World is one reason why overseas church leaders are
puzzled by the efforts of some U.S. mission leaders to
send more evangelistic missionaries overseas. They ask,
"How can people who are seeing a decline in membership in their own churches help us in evangelism?"
When these church leaders in the Third World continue to read of certain mission agencies talking of the
need to reach the heathen in Africa or Asia, they begin
to raise questions about integrity: "Are such appeals
made out of a real concern for the gospel," they ask, "or
to raise money for a particular organization?" This has
been one of the underlying reasons for a call for a moratorium.

It is important to understand these growing churches
in terms more instructive than mere statistics. For
many years now, indigenous church leaders have felt
that Western missionaries were not the best evangelists
for their areas. At first it was not because the missionary
was disliked or because of the other problems mentioned earlier. It was because the missionary could
never fully enter into the local culture.

I vividly remember a visit to an inland West African
city while working with the American Bible Society. My
colleague and I first stopped at a mission station only to

find the atmosphere among the missionaries so tense that luncheon was eaten almost in silence. We did learn that there were problems between the church and the mission over which one should do evangelism work in the unreached areas surrounding this small provincial city. After lunch and discussion of Bible Society business we drove in to town and met with the president of the church, who was the local pastor.

Our discussion was friendly but clouded by unstated difficulties. Finally we told him about our visit with the missionaries and of their concern over the tension with the church. "Did they tell you why?" the pastor asked. We replied that we understood the issue to be over who should evangelize the unreached peoples in the area. He nodded his agreement.

"But why should there be a problem over who should do evangelism?" we asked. That question opened the floodgates of pent-up emotion. He told a story of how the mission had a policy that the church should look after the internal affairs of the church and that the mission should be engaged in evangelistic endeavors. The pastor then told us why he felt that the church should be doing evangelism.

"For years the missionaries have been going to a village about sixty kilometers from here. It is a village with a strong witch doctor and they have never seen one person brought to Jesus Christ despite all their efforts. I tried reasoning with them. In view of the difficulties they had experienced in that particular village—and to help reach a better understanding between us about why we in the church should be about evangelism—I suggested that they permit me to go to that village in place of one of their missionaries when the next visit was scheduled.

"When the day came, I went alone to the village. As I approached, the witch doctor came out to meet me. We met at the edge of the village and he asked me why I had come. I told him that I had come in place of the missionary to tell the people about Jesus Christ. At that point something happened which no missionary had ever experienced: the witch doctor took his stick and drew a line across the path between us. He looked at me and said: 'You cross that line and you will die.' For some time I argued with him—long enough for most of the people in the village to gather round and understand what the argument was about.

"Finally, when most of the people had assembled round us, I looked at the witch doctor and said: 'I know you have the power to kill me. I have known of you for many years and have heard many stories of your powers. I am no foreigner. I am a man of this people and I know the source of your power. But I am also a Christian. I believe that Jesus Christ is the Son of the all-powerful God. I believe that he has greater power than you. I have come to tell your people about the good news of Jesus Christ, and because he is more powerful than you I am going to step across your line. I will not die, for your power is nothing compared to the power of Jesus Christ whom I serve.' I then stepped across the line, walked with the people into the village and told them of Jesus Christ. The witch doctor had lost face in front of the people of his village. Many of them believed and confessed Christ that day. Now we have a church in that village."

That experience instructed my understanding of evangelism in Africa. Every people understand and believe in terms of their culture. The gospel can only be effectively communicated in the context of a people's culture. Once the church in Africa, in Asia, and in other lands is free to be itself and to reach out in the context of its own understanding of Christ and its culture, growth in the church follows that witness.

In most of these churches there is a naturalness about an individual's witness to Christ. Witness is not a cultivated characteristic; it is as natural as talking politics.

The United Presbyterian Church of North America had carried on mission work in Ethiopia before the Italian invasion in 1935. There were scattered communities of Christians but there was no organized church. During the war the missionaries were repatriated. The small evangelical Christian communities were left to face alone both the Italian invaders and persecution at the hands of the Ethiopian Orthodox Church. When peace came in 1941, returning missionaries found a church that had grown in their absence. It had ordained pastors and a sense of being a community of Christian believers. It also felt a responsibility for reaching out to the areas in which its people lived.

Kais Gidada, one of the pastors of the church, tells of the coming of the first representative of the mission after the peace. The visitor asked what help the church in America could give them now that the missionaries were free to come back. Gidada writes: "We told him that he might help us by asking the church in America to send doctors and teachers to train leaders for the church, and some dressers for the people's health."[29] It is notable that there was no request for evangelists. The church had discovered itself and its own ability to witness to the Lordship of Jesus Christ.

The church in Korea also has rightfully earned a reputation for being a witnessing church. It has emphasized evangelism as its first priority and ordered its life accordingly. Since 1900, when the church was in its infancy, it had grown to 3 million members by 1970, something over 10 percent of the South Korean population. The following story taken from the 1975 report of the representative of the United Presbyterian Church in Korea indicates the spirit that pervades this church.

" 'Sodom' was the call name for a little village in the outer suburbs of Andong. For centuries it was an open secret that the wealthy men came there to carouse with wine and women. In early 1975 the women of the Andong Presbyterian Church decided that God wanted them to change that village. For several months the salvation message was proclaimed and just before Christmas a lovely new church was dedicated and 'Sodom' had been transformed into a 'New Community'!"[30]

Another story from the same report tells the following: "In 1975 . . . a rural church in 'Silent Valley' was dedicated in memory of an unusually bountiful man, Kim Soo-man, a leg amputee. After making his own peg leg, Elder Kim, carrying a cane in one hand and a Bible and a hymnbook in the other, spent thirty years visiting unchurched villages in his mountainous country. Come wind, come weather, until his death recently, he was the greatest evangelist in the 'Korean Highlands.' Soo-man led hundreds and hundreds of mountain people to faith in Jesus Christ. In establishing ten churches, which are now all self-supporting, he probably accomplished more than any other Christian I know in an effective method of planting new churches."[31]

The stories could be continued. They add up to one fact: God is moving through the Holy Spirit to establish the church. And God is doing it through the faithful witness of simple Christians in Indonesia, Brazil, Ghana,

and in almost every other place where the church of
Jesus Christ has taken root as a result of the modern
missionary movement.

The Independent Church Movement

So far we have been discussing churches that were
founded as a result of Western missionary work. It is
these churches which we have been alluding to as national or indigenous churches.

There is another group of churches that need to be
introduced if the total sweep of what God is doing
through the church is to be understood. Throughout
the world there is the phenomenon of the "breakaway"
or "independent" churches. These are churches that
are the result of some individual's leaving a mission-
established church and starting a totally independent
church without any external support.

In Africa more than five thousand such movements
have been identified by Barrett in his book *Schism and
Renewal in Africa.*[32] This phenomenon started in 1862
and is still continuing. Some independent churches may
consist of only one congregation; others may have four
or five congregations. The largest have a million or
more members scattered over several countries.

Barrett believes that this group of churches is Christian. Other breakaway groups have lost the central core
of Christian belief, but we are not discussing those. According to 1970 statistics, there are nine million members of the Independent Churches in Africa. It is es-
timated by Barrett that in the year A.D. 2000 there will
be 34 million members of these churches. Obviously it
is important to give attention to why these churches
grow.

These churches are called "independent" not only because they are free of external control. They are, more importantly, independent because they receive no subsidy and no missionaries. In Ghana, where I have had the greatest contact with independent churches, it has been interesting to note how they differ from mission-funded churches. There is a high degree of concern about individual members and their needs. Every day the leaders have "counseling periods," during which members come to talk about their problems. One man may have lost his job. There will be prayer that God will open up a new position. But rarely does the counseling stop there. A frank discussion of the family's financial predicament will follow. If real need exists, the leader gives help from his "bishop's bag."

A woman will come seeking prayer that she may have a child. Barrenness in Africa is as serious a problem as it was in Old Testament times. There will be prayer and perhaps anointing with oil. Later, at a special meeting of the congregation all the women who are seeking God's blessing so that they may have children will come forward. They will be publicly questioned as to their marital faithfulness. They will also be asked whether they are prepared to raise the children that God may give them in the Christian way. Then there will be laying on of hands and prayer.

At another point in the same service, women who sought help in this way and later gave birth to children will come forward to have their children consecrated to God's service. The two separate parts of the same service are impressive because in Africa it would be very hard to fool such an audience. The people know one another well, they have long memories, and the leader is not itinerant but is a stable part of the community.

The above illustrations are stated in some detail to give an idea of the concerned community which composes an independent church. No problem is turned away. Each is dealt with in prayer *and* in practical ways wherever the resources are available.

Barrett points out that one of the reformatory themes in the independent churches is "the emphasis on *philadelphia,* brotherly love, [which is] seen as the Christian version of African traditional values of . . . community, group solidarity, hospitality,"[33] and one should add, the extended family. In traditional African society, the extended family is as meaningful and real as the nuclear family in the West. No family member is ever turned away when in need no matter how distant the relationship.

Mission-founded churches have largely lost this emphasis because of the imposition of Western theology and its Western cultural assumptions on these churches. The independent churches have been free to develop their own expression of the Christian faith in the context of African culture.

Worship in the independent churches will vary greatly, but one can generally count on the use of drums, tambourines, clapping, and indigenous African instruments. With the natural rhythm and beat of such music, rhythmic dancing is generally a part of worship. The offering is almost always received to the accompaniment of a rhythmic dance as the worshipers bring forward their offerings to lay them on the Communion table.

Some leaders of these movements are otherwise employed, so that they are not an expense to the church. However, increasingly congregations desire a full-time leader in order to provide the counseling service mentioned above. Therefore, the members support the church in a manner that will provide a salary for the leader.

I have never had the feeling that these churches are opposed to external support. They simply have never received any and don't count on it. Visitors from Western churches are received with honor and frequently given gifts. On my first visit to one of the churches in Accra, Ghana, I arrived at a time when the leader was engaged in counseling his people. He received me graciously, told me something of his ministry, invited me to return for one of the services. As I was about to leave he asked me to wait. He went into his home, and soon returned with a sealed envelope which he handed me. Later when I opened the envelope I found that it contained an autographed photograph and the equal of almost thirty-four U.S. dollars in local currency. He had asked for nothing from me. I was his guest and African custom requires that something be shared with a guest. Generally a guest is invited to a meal, but that was not possible at the time I came. What I received was his way of breaking bread with me.

The one thing that most independent church leaders seek is Bible training. On the whole they are not highly educated people and lack formal theological education. They claim—and their lives generally show—that God has given them gifts of healing, preaching, and other ministries. Not all independent church leaders are reputable. Some suffer from weaknesses common to humanity. It is probable that the percentage of those who stumble may not be much greater than is the case with leaders in mission-founded churches. Considering the tremendous influence wielded by independent church leaders within their congregations, that comparison is significant.

But What About the 2.7 Billion Unreached?

"More than 2,700 million people, which is more than two thirds of mankind, have yet to be evangelized. We are ashamed that so many have been neglected; it is a standing rebuke to the whole church."[34]

What has been said earlier about the tremendous growth of the church in the Third World needs to be seen in the light of this statement from the Lausanne Covenant. The rate of growth of the churches becomes less significant when one realizes that the worldwide Christian community comprises only one third of the world's population.

It is important, however, that the 2.7 billion figure be studied to determine its composition and distribution regarding proximity to established, growing churches. The same statistics by Ralph Winter that give us the total of 2.7 billion unreached also provide us with a geographical breakdown of both Christians and non-Christians:[35]

	Christians millions	Non-Christians millions
West: Europe, Latin and North America	965	327
Africa	116	282
Asia	98	2,114

	Christians ratio	*Non-Christians* ratio
West: Europe, Latin and North America	1	0.34
Africa	1	2.4
Asia	1	21.6

Winter's figures are projections to 1975. He predicts that by A.D. 2000 the ratio of Christians to non-Christians in Africa will be 1 to 1.2. This prediction is based on the rapid growth of the African churches. What is not taken into consideration by these figures is the concentration of the Christian population in sub-Saharan Africa; only about 7 percent of Africa's Christians live in North Africa. This means that the ratio in sub-Saharan Africa would be changed substantially in the direction of numerical equality of Christians with non-Christians.

The church in Africa south of the Sahara, along with the church in West Africa, is not overwhelmed by non-Christian neighbors. In both areas the church should be able to deal effectively with the matter of evangelization. The same could be said of certain areas of Asia.

The truly unreached areas of Africa and Asia are those where the Muslim faith is dominant (664 million), the places where the people follow Hinduism (502 million), and the Chinese community (827 million). These vast communities of the world's peoples account for two billion of the unreached. The remainder are 403 million who are the neighbors of the African-Asian churches; and 327 million who are the neighbors of the churches that Winter calls "the West"—Europe, Latin America, and North America.

To break down the oft-quoted figure of 2.7 billion unreached into its component parts helps to avoid distortion of the basic question of this study. The Christian church indeed has a responsibility to witness to the good news of God's Kingdom as revealed by our Lord to all who have not heard. But the cause of God's Kingdom is not well served if matters are confused by our failing to recognize where the missionary movement's work has been successful in establishing the church and where it has been clearly unsuccessful. Winter, in this connection, says: "Most missionaries and most mission boards may hope someone else will worry about the special problem of winning Muslims, Hindus, and Chinese, since these have historically been the most resistant to the gospel."[36]

The matter of these three communities that make up the unreached two billion is important enough for us to take it up in more detail in the final chapter. For now, the matter can be summarized by noting that these two billion unreached are going to require a very special effort—a new movement of God's Spirit. Besides these, there are 700 million others who are the neighbors of vital churches in Africa and Asia—and our neighbors in the Western world. The churches in Africa and Asia are clearly doing their part in evangelizing their neighbors. How effective are we in witnessing to *our* neighbors?

QUESTIONS FOR DISCUSSION

1. The growth of churches in Africa, according to Latourette, has been going on for three decades. The

quotation from Winter suggests that the rate of growth has increased in recent years. What have you known about these developments? How do they compare with growth in your local church? in your denomination?

2. When you think of a missionary, what kind of work do you envision? Did the reply quoted by Kais Gidada surprise you? In view of what you have read about a Christian witness being most effective when communicated in a culturally relevant manner, has your view of the missionary changed?

3. What is your response to the style of worship in the African independent churches? Why do we think an organ or a piano is more worshipful than drums and clapping? Does the answer for Americans not tend to reflect their culture?

4. How does the independent churches' emphasis on *philadelphia,* brotherly love, compare with the early Christian fellowship recorded in Acts? How do the members of your congregation express this concern for one another?

5. Winter points out that there are 403 million people in Africa and Asia who are not Christian, Muslim, Hindu, or in the Chinese community. How many Western missionaries do you think are at work among the 403 million? How many are working among the two billion Muslim, Hindu, and Chinese? After you agree on the two figures, jot them down for later comparison with Winter's figures noted in Chapter 6.

4

Mission and Justice

Justice is basic to the renewal of the Christian mission. So far we have only touched upon this issue. For Americans who enjoy the greatest affluence of any nation in history, justice may not rank high on our agenda. It may shock us to learn that it is primary for most people in the Third World.

It may be even more of a shock for us to learn that tolerance of things as they are is running low all around the world. This feeling was well expressed by Martin Luther King, Jr., in a letter he wrote from the Birmingham jail to eight clergymen who criticized him. He said: "History is the long and tragic story of the fact that privileged groups seldom give up their unjust posture. . . . We know through painful experience that freedom is never voluntarily given by the oppressor; it must be demanded by the oppressed."[37]

There are those who take the point of view that men like Dr. King are disturbers of the peace: Had he remained quiet, demonstrations such as those which occurred in Birmingham would never have happened. The issue is not a new one. The British Quaker, John Bright, faced it squarely in the Parliament in 1866 when he said:

"I have never said a word in favor of force. All I have said has been against it—but I am at liberty to warn those in authority that justice long delayed, or long continued injustice, provokes the employment of force to obtain redress. It is in the ordering of nature and therefore of the supreme that this is so, and all preaching to the contrary is of no avail.

"If men build houses on the slopes of a Vesuvius, I may tell them of their folly and insecurity, but I am not in any way provoking, or responsible for, the eruption which sweeps them all away. I may say too that force to prevent freedom and to deny rights is not more moral than force to gain freedom and secure rights."[38]

It is important to marshal these arguments for the cause of justice because most Americans seem to have lost their sensitivity to injustice. They cannot understand when people rise up to fight for freedom in the 1970's, forgetting that we did precisely the same two centuries ago. Julius Nyerere, president of Tanzania, stated the case bluntly when he wrote: "A man can change his religion if he wishes; he can accept a different political belief—or in both cases give appearance of doing so—if this would relieve him of intolerable circumstances. But no man can change his colour or his race. And if he suffers because of it, he must either become less than a man or he must fight. And for good or evil, mankind has been created that many will refuse to acquiesce in their own degradation; they will destroy peace rather than suffer under it."[39]

It is in this context that the issue of *justice* has become a significant part of mission in our day. Justice has always been a part of the mission of God's people, although a part that is easy to forget when we are materi-

ally blessed. In Amos, God speaks through the prophet
to the affluent people of that day:

> I hate, I despise your feasts,
>   and I take no delight in your solemn
>   assemblies,
> Even though you offer me your burnt offerings
>   and cereal offerings,
>   I will not accept them,
> and the peace offerings of your fatted beasts
>   I will not look upon.
> Take away from me the noise of your songs;
>   to the melody of your harps I will not listen.
> But let justice roll down like waters,
>   and righteousness like an ever-flowing stream.
>   (Amos 5:21–24)

The Most Guilty Man . . . Is Every One of Us

In Chapter 2 we saw something of the problems
created by the superior attitude, racism, and economic
privilege which had developed in the missionary community. While it is important that these issues be understood, it is more important that we do not project these
faults solely onto the missionary community. Orlando
E. Costas, Secretary of Studies and Publications, Insti-
tute of In-Depth Evangelism in Latin America, gives us
a clue to the source of the problem:

"This tendency may be seen not just among the missionaries. In a sense, the latter are no more and no less
a reflection of the attitudes and overall philosophy of
the missionary societies, church, and individual Christians who sent them. Having lived and studied in North
America, I can understand how so many missionaries
can think and act the way they do. . . . They are a part

of a syncretistic religious culture. I say syncretistic because many of the values inherent in this culture are definitely not Christian. Yet, they have been made to appear as if they were. Worse yet, these values have permeated the mental structure of the great majority of Christians in the North Atlantic."[40]

About ten years ago I was talking with an African friend about developments in African theology. We began to discuss the problem of syncretism—the attempt to reconcile the Western and African philosophical bases of theology. He expressed concern that Western theologians would condemn African theology as syncretistic. As we discussed this problem a light seemed to dawn in his thinking. He said: "You Americans are syncretistic: you worship two gods. You worship God, the Father of our Lord Jesus Christ, and you also worship the American dollar."

Frankly I never fully understood the meaning of that remark until I began to put it into the context of this issue of justice. What my friend in Africa saw that night, Costas saw as he lived among us. He tells us that the missionaries who go out from our churches reflect our failure to allow the gospel to renew our lives and witness in our own nation.

This point is so important and so difficult for us to understand that we may need to try to see it from another perspective. In 1949 the Communist armies under Mao Tse-tung defeated the nationalists and ended the missionary era in China. Several thoughtful books have been written about the missions in China in the light of the Communist take-over. In one of these books the Rev. David M. Paton, a former British missionary to China, deals at length with two issues that seriously negated the Christian witness in China: race

and economics. Because these issues are central to the
matter of justice, for most Western peoples they must
be faced squarely.

Paton believes that racial prejudice is the most important issue in the world as a whole, and that the core
of the race problem emerges in our attitudes toward
the mixed marriage. We have to be clear what we think
about that.

Most white Christians like to think they have passed
the test when it comes to racism. But interracial marriage tends to rouse deep feelings in most of us, proving
that we have actually failed the final examination.
Paton points out that the Chinese are not much interested in marrying people of other races. I have found
this to be true also in Africa. However, because people
of darker skin have suffered so long from white racial
prejudice, there cannot be compromise of any kind on
this subject. If we believe that all who have named
Christ as Savior are truly one, then there is no place for
racial prejudice in any form.

Paton admonishes that the place for most of us to start
is not to demand broader attitudes among missionaries
or other white men overseas, but to ensure that the
many Africans and others from overseas who come here
to study or work are made to feel at home, "which not
infrequently means being invited into your home and
mine."

Concerning the issue of money, Paton indicates that
when he was in China he was paid about three times as
much as a Chinese of comparable age and responsibility
in the church. He admits that it is very difficult to get
this problem into perspective and to avoid both senti-
mentality and hardheartedness. But it is very important
to do so, because too many missionaries have had a

guilty conscience for years, and a guilty conscience is inhibiting and frustrating.

The matter of money is even more serious for American missionaries. Paton only alludes to the "American colleague handling those world-coveted U.S. dollars." In fact, American missionaries are often paid at a rate that is double or three times that of their European counterparts. Our style of life in America is infectious and those of us who go abroad tend to carry it with us —at great cost both to the supporting constituency and to our witness.

It is on "the frontier" where our life-style and that of another people inevitably come together that the issue of justice is joined. For Paton the matter could be handled in only one way: "The conclusion is that where the manner of life constitutes a bar to full fellowship, manner of life must be altered; and that on the evidence, we should be chary of a facile assumption that differing manners of life do not create such barriers."[41]

On the issue of race, Paton writes as a Britisher and speaks to the sins of his own people. How much greater our American sin! I shall never forget listening, in Africa, to the radio during the years of the civil rights movement. Every newscast would start with what the whites were doing to the blacks in the Southern States. It would tell of the use of police dogs, water hoses, and guns; the arrogant rejection of black students' attempts to enter the then all-white schools. White American violence toward black Americans, terrible as it was on the American scene, took on far greater dimensions of horror in Africa. "Why," African friends asked, "had the church not changed these attitudes?" It was in Ghana that I most vividly remember the impact of those radio broadcasts. Thinking back on those days, I have often wondered what part those developments had in turning some of the leaders of Africa, like Kwame Nkrumah, then president of Ghana, away from the West.

Or consider our treatment of overseas students studying in our American universities. Few may realize that the so-called politburo in Ethiopia, the political advisers to the provisional military government, is made up of men who studied in the West. They are all Marxists. One of these advisers studied at the University of Syracuse in New York. He told an Ethiopian friend that his experience in America, his rejection because of his color and the affluent manner in which we live, left him with no option but to reject our whole economic system, which he feels is at the root of our attitudes.

There are those among us who, beginning to understand something of the problem that our way of life is creating in the world, talk in a way similar to the Ethiopian who studied at Syracuse. They are not Marxists, they are loyal Americans. But as they begin to feel some of the weight of the matters mentioned above, they tend to strike out at "the system." With that attitude we cannot get very far with the issue of justice.

Prof. David Bosch, dean of the Faculty of Theology at the University of South Africa, has spoken clearly to this point out of his own personal experience within his country. He warns of a pervasive danger "that all the guilt from the wrongs of society can be located solely *outside* the church. Let me illustrate what I mean: The clearest expression of religious dissent in Russia comes from *Samizdat,* a clandestine Christian publication. More than half a million Russians work for this organization in their free time. An important message, recurring in *Samizdat,* is that every man, and particularly every Christian, is responsible for the sociopolitical shortcomings of his society. Thus, instead of attacking the 'system' and blaming it for all maladies, *Samizdat* addresses itself to the conscience of individual Christians with the message: 'We declare that the most guilty man, responsible for the wrong doings of society, is every one of us.' "[42]

If we can adopt this attitude, there will be renewal in the Christian mission. So long as we are part of the American affluent society, and accept its privileges, "the most guilty man, responsible for the wrong doings of society, is every one of us."

South Africa

The fact that Bosch speaks as he does is in no small part because he belongs to white South African society. Furthermore, he is an Afrikaner—the people who make up the base of support for the current ruling Nationalist Party. The Nationalist Party has been in power since 1948. The Afrikaner leadership, having fought the British for control of the country, was determined not to lose it to the black majority of the South African population. Their determination to maintain white control of the country resulted in the policy of *apartheid*—an Afrikaans word meaning separate development.

According to apartheid, each of the major African tribes would be given a "homeland" which would eventually become independent of South Africa—nations where the African peoples could exercise rule. The purpose of apartheid was to ensure that white rule of the remainder of South Africa would not be threatened. The problem with this Nationalist solution to the racial issue in South Africa is that the whites, who make up about 18 percent of South Africa's population, intend to keep about 86 percent of the land and almost all its minerals. This would leave the blacks of the country, who make up 72 percent of the population, with less than 14 percent of the land.

While many arguments can be adduced for the Afrikaner position—some of them perfectly valid—the overall policy is doomed because of the obvious injustice of the plan. The blacks of South Africa suffer under this injustice and, to quote Nyerere again, "a man . . . must either become less than a man or he must fight." As this book is being written, the fighting has begun. Because this revolution will be of more than local concern, it is important to try to understand some of the issues at stake.

One needs to start with a basic fact: the South African problem does not lend itself to simple solutions. The white population is as much a part of Africa as the white population of North America. White settlement began in both areas at roughly the same time. To call South Africa a colonial issue is a misuse of words.

The Afrikaner people have a deep sense of identification with whites in America. Like us, they fought the British, who at one time were the colonial power in South Africa as they were in America. The British won that war but later they lost the peace. The Afrikaner people took over by political struggle what they lost through armed struggle. Afrikaners created South Africa through pioneering and hard work even as America was created out of the wilderness. One could extend the similarities; but there are also significant differences.

Afrikaners, who came out of Dutch stock, are a clannish people. They take their history and their Calvinist religion seriously. They had no alternative but to accept

the white English people who were already in the country. But the Afrikaner resisted the kind of immigration
that America experienced from all over Europe. For
that reason the white population grew much more
slowly than did the white population of North America.

At the time that the Afrikaner was settling South
Africa, the African people, who had for years been mi-
grating southward, were also moving in large numbers
into the area now known as South Africa. Inevitably,
both the Afrikaner settlers and the English colonial
forces came into conflict with the African people. Several wars were fought between white and black. Eventually the superior arms of the whites defeated the
blacks and they became a subject people.

Afrikaners point out that white and black learned to
live in peace in South Africa. They contrast this with the
fact that in North America the whites killed and drove
out the Indians, so that they no longer pose a threat to
us. Let that judgment stand for the truth that is in it.
The one thing that the Afrikaner does not mention is
that the African peoples whom they conquered had no
alternative at the time but to accept defeat. It was a
peace imposed by a conqueror. Until World War II,
while the Western powers ruled the world, the conquered peoples of South Africa remained in subjection.
They were never made indentured slaves, but neither
did they have any rights. After the war, the liberation
movements of Africa eventually found sources of arms
—the Marxist countries of Eastern Europe.

The common theology of the Afrikaner people was
that as descendants of Ham, the blacks were con-
demned to be "hewers of wood and drawers of water."
Generally speaking, the blacks were considered to be
superior to animals but certainly not equal with whites.

This extreme form of racism carried throughout most of the white community until the time of the civil rights movement in the United States. Before that time certain black leaders of South Africa began to organize political parties hoping to gain human rights for their people in the same manner as the Afrikaners had achieved victory—through political means. But quickly these efforts were thwarted by the outlawing of all black political parties.

The early tensions that resulted from these developments brought the leaders of the Dutch Reformed Church to restudy their theology, and gradually the "curse on Ham" interpretation was rejected. Several other approaches were attempted to defend Scripturally white superiority. Each of these followed the "curse on Ham" theology into the scrap heap of false theological premises. When the Afrikaners found no Scriptural defense for their support of white control, they fell back on the political dictum of apartheid. The issue of justice was rarely raised within the church—and not at all in political life.

An American reading this account may feel that the white South Africans are heartless people. That judgment may be premature.

Because the white community in South Africa is comparatively small, the Europeanization of the country has taken time and come through hard effort. Today, most whites live a good life. The white farms have been developed to much the same level as those in the American Midwest, except that black labor is used in place of mechanization. The business centers of the large cities are surrounded by comfortable white suburbs. Behind the scenes in every business establishment are the black workers. In almost every white home are several servants who cook, clean, do the laundry, and care for the garden. Black wages are so low that almost every white family can afford to have black servants.

In recent years South Africa has attempted to show its better side by emphasizing how much black wages have increased. The tragic, unmentioned fact is that the gap between white and black wages has widened even further during this period. Comparisons are, on the whole, not too meaningful, because whites do not do house or garden work for pay. Most blacks in this kind of work are barely able to buy food, pay for rent and transportation to the place of employment, in addition to buying a few "luxuries" such as clothing. Many cannot afford to send their children to school, because schooling for blacks is not free. Schooling for white children is free. Where comparisons can be made, as for example in the teaching profession, the salary of a white teacher may be four times the salary of a black teacher.

On the white farms where almost one third of the black South Africans live, life is very much as it was in the American South after the Civil War. A black family remains essentially bound to a white farmer, because the family cannot gain sufficient capital to move away. Often the family will be continuously in debt to the farmer, who keeps wages so low that borrowing becomes a way of life. Schooling for the children of these black families is at the discretion of the white farmers. They may provide some form of education if they are so inclined; they do not have to do so legally.

Another one third of black South Africans live in the so-called homelands. Recently these areas began to be developed in order to give credence to the policy of apartheid. Essentially they exist to provide migrant labor for the mines and certain industries of the large white cities. Generally speaking, there are comparatively few able-bodied men in these homelands. One usually finds only women, children, and older people. The economy of the area has depended almost entirely on the wages of the men who go to the white areas as migrant laborers. This is beginning to change with more recent homeland development, but the change is almost glacial and the historic patterns still prevail.

It is the other third of the blacks, who live in the urban areas, and who are the workers, that make the South African economy what it is and make the white South African life-styles so comfortable. As already noted, they are paid comparatively little for the work they do—and the disparity is based entirely on the color of a person's skin, not on ability.

But beyond that, the urban blacks must live, as it were, "out of sight." In Johannesburg, for example, the best-known black community is Soweto. In Soweto about a million black people live in simple four-room houses, mostly without electricity or running water. Such a house may have to accommodate as many as ten persons. The Soweto community is situated in such a way that its transportation and roads lead only to the white city. Each day those who live in Soweto rise before dawn and ride the train or bus to their work. There they do the bidding of the whites. When the day has ended, they return to their community aboard the same crowded transport to face an evening with few diversions.

All of this says little about the dread that every urban African faces because of a series of laws passed by the white government to protect its interests. There are laws that govern the conditions under which an African can live in an urban community. All too frequently these laws end up separating husband and wife and destroying families. There are laws that give the government power to punish blacks who have gotten out of line by having said something that threatens the white power structure. Blacks can be "banned" (a modern, political form of leprosy) if they join a protest movement. There is also a law that demands that a black person carry a "pass book" in which is recorded all the person's vital statistics, police record, work record, and any other information the police may wish to record. It is referred to frequently as the "book of life." If anyone is found without this book, the person is subject to immediate arrest and imprisonment.

Perhaps the greatest indignity of all are the police raids on black homes. Any night, at any hour, the police may knock on a door without a warrant, ransack the house, and take away anything and anyone in it. The person can be held in prison indefinitely, without charges. Such tactics keep the black community in a state of insecurity—which is precisely the purpose.

On May 8, 1976, the Anglican dean of Johannesburg, the Rev. Desmond Tutu, a black South African, wrote a letter to the prime minister of his country. It began with a word of appreciation for the prime minister's intervention on his behalf to obtain a South African passport which had enabled him to take up a post as Associate Director for Africa of the Theological Education Fund. The letter continued with the very human appeal which is common to all: to the mutual love of children, the pride of fatherhood, the love of a husband. He then went on to say:

"I am writing to you, Sir, as one who is a member of a race that has known what is meant in frustration and hurts, in agony and humiliation, to be a subject people

... because, like you, I am deeply committed to a real reconciliation with justice for all and to peaceful change to a more just and open South African society in which the wonderful riches and wealth of our country will be shared more equitably . . . because I have a growing nightmarish fear that unless something drastic is done very soon, then bloodshed and violence are going to happen in South Africa almost inevitably. A people can take only so much and no more."

For five full pages Dean Tutu poured out his heart to the white leader of his country. He asked that something be done, and soon, to indicate to the black community of South Africa that the white community seriously sought to change the pattern of oppression which South African society had imposed upon the blacks. In a brief reply the prime minister accused Dean Tutu of making "propaganda."[43]

Before we form the judgment that the Afrikaner people are heartless, we must see them as they see themselves. Their backs are against the wall trying to preserve the way of life which they have worked so hard to achieve. We also need to understand that they count heavily on United States military support should they get into trouble.

It may seem strange to the average American to think of our nation defending a people whose racial policies are such as have just been described. But South Africa has other factors going for it. In economic terms, American industry controls about 20 percent of the foreign investment in South Africa. While that investment is not large in comparison with our total African and worldwide investment, it is profitable because of the low labor cost and superficial political stability. South Africa is also the source of many vital minerals needed in the Western world. Even more important is the South African control of the "Cape route," the ocean passage around the Cape of Good Hope used by most of the supertankers carrying oil from Arabia to the United States and other Western countries. The Cape route is also the Atlantic approach to the Indian Ocean —an area now being contested by the Soviet Union. The fear that the Soviet Union might establish a naval base on what is now South African territory, following the triumph of a Soviet-armed black liberation struggle, has led most military strategists to the conviction that the West must control access to that area at all costs.

So despite our official condemnation of South Africa's racial policies, we continue to cooperate in strategic areas. That cooperation led former Secretary of State Henry Kissinger to make a belated effort to help resolve the Rhodesian conflict. At the heart of that plan was the indemnification of white Rhodesians for any loss that might occur through black rule. The plan had its merits. But who can deny the black African charge that America was trying to save the white people, at the point of their collapse, in order to avoid a Marxist military take-over such as occurred in Angola?

And why did the United States wait so long? For years the blacks of Rhodesia have cried out for justice. Six million blacks have been ruled by 275,000 whites and our nation has shown little concern. Only when a Marxist take-over was threatening did we become interested. Is it any wonder that the African people ask: Why so late and why reward the whites, who have caused us so much suffering?

The black-ruled nations of Africa wonder about our attitudes. Can it be that race and economic interests dictate our diplomatic concerns in Africa? If so, why do we condemn the whites of South Africa, who are also looking out for their racial and economic interests?

The lack of human rights for blacks in southern Africa is one of the most serious diplomatic questions facing the U.S. Government. What sort of influence will the members of the church in America bring to bear upon that question? Each one of us, some perhaps only in a limited way, profits from the exploitation of black labor in southern white-ruled Africa. Each one of us has an opportunity to express our concern over the situation in southern Africa to our elected representatives. As church members we could be an effective voice for justice in this difficult problem area of the world if we are truly concerned.

Yet, on the whole, few in the church who are concerned for its mission have thought very much about those who cry for justice. In a later chapter the implications of our attitudes on the witness of the church will be considered further. For now we need to go back to the statement from *Samizdat*. Do we really believe it is true that "the most guilty man, responsible for the wrong doings of society, is every one of us"?

QUESTIONS FOR DISCUSSION

1. What have you previously thought about the liberation movements in Africa? In what way does the background given in this chapter put the issues in a different perspective? How do African desires for equality and justice differ from American desires in 1776?

2. The quotation from Costas shifts the blame for the faults found in missionaries from them alone to all of

us in the church. Do you think he is right? Why or why not? What changes do we need to make in our lives and witness in each of our congregations?

3. Cite specific instances in which money or the things money can buy inhibit our faithfulness to Christ. When it comes to our *disposable* income, what priority do we give to our concern for others?

4. David Paton makes two points about the failure of missionary workers in China. What is your attitude toward interracial marriage? How do our life-styles show our concern for others?

5. As a people who cherish our democratic freedoms, what can we do to extend freedom to others? What are the perils of affluence in regard to our response to the cries of the oppressed for justice? Are other ideologies winning the battle for the minds of Third World people? Why do you think so?

6. Ecologists tell us that we are already threatening future generations by the way we live. If this is true, what does justice for the dispossessed of the world mean for us?

5

The Call for a Moratorium

"The simple truth about the moratorium is that we, African Christians, have no desire to be the channel through which the continued domination of Africa is assured."[44]

Chapter 1 mentioned the call for a moratorium and some of the problems that lay behind it. The issues it raises, however, are so complicated and so significant for the missionary enterprise that a more comprehensive review is needed.

Search for Understanding

The plea to stop sending missionaries, together with other issues related to overseas mission, has caused deep and serious discussion within the denominations. Our own communion has sought to hear what our related churches around the world were saying to us about mission today. Teams composed of board members and staff were mandated to travel to five geographical areas, two by two, to listen to what the churches were saying. I participated in the team that traveled to Africa in February and March of 1975.

We did not ask the obvious question: "Do you want

a moratorium?" Rather, we told our African colleagues of the discussions and debates going on within our church and that we were visiting to listen to what they had to say to us about these matters and any others. Almost without exception the first thing they wanted to talk about was moratorium. With only one exception, no one with whom we talked supported the idea as stated at Lusaka and apparently none of them had voted for it. The churches we visited were not ready to request moratorium. Many of them opposed the idea in principle; others felt that it was too harshly stated; still others felt it was premature.

The one church that wholeheartedly supported the idea is in a unique position by its own evaluation. It is a church in South Africa with a comparatively strong economic base and with only a few missionaries in its midst.

Some churches apparently had not as yet studied the matter officially. The persons with whom we talked were clearly speaking only for themselves and perhaps their executive committees. Comments ranged from "In twenty years everybody will support it" to "Moratorium is something which people who don't have enough work to do can sit and discuss."

I came away from the discussions with the feeling that the churches of Africa which came into being as a result of Western missionary work have a deep symbiotic relationship to our churches and that the tearing of that relationship will not come easily.

That realization did not give a great deal of comfort. The struggles of Western Christendom which resulted in our denominational dividedness have no intrinsic meaning for most Africans. These reflections of our struggles—and our sinfulness—do not relate to African problems or contribute to their understanding of the gospel. We have exported our divisions because they are apparently important to us; but they are *our* divisions. It is the gospel of our Lord Jesus Christ which has brought meaning to our African friends, not our divisions.

Our relationships, therefore, seem to be rooted more in history and in our contribution of people and funds than in anything much deeper. If that evaluation is correct, I find it troubling. It is out of those factors that the main issues of moratorium arise: the issues of domination and dependence.

Captive Relationships

The parent-child relationship which forms the basis of far too much Western mission work is fraught with dangers. The superior-inferior status of the related churches is nearly inevitable. When such a relationship is maintained by perpetuating past policies, the relationship can be destructive to both parties. Only if a new relationship can be developed which is based on love and community can the future be considered hopeful.

In this context the call for a moratorium out of Lusaka is a rebellion against the continuing domination of certain missionaries and Western mission agencies. It reveals the developing understanding of some African Christians that their people have grown dependent and lack full maturity as followers of Jesus Christ. They want something better.

For Western churches, what has been called the "mother-daughter" relationship has been so much a part of our mission thinking that it has received far too little critical attention. The very statement of the relationship should be cause for concern. Yet until recently the "mother-daughter" language has been used without concern for its inherent spiritual superiority on the part of the so-called "mother" church.

But the problem almost universally goes beyond language. In many instances the former "mother" church continues to act, at least subconsciously, as if it knew what is best for "their daughter" church. In too many such relationships today no obvious effort is being made to establish new forms of relationship. Either the "mother-daughter" relationship is too comfortable or the effort to establish a new relationship is too painful.

There is a sentence from the report of the Ecumenical Sharing of Personnel meeting which captures this insight quite well: "Moratorium is understood to be a process of liberation from captive relationships."[45]

Economic Realities

Another factor underlying the call for a moratorium has been the recent reduction in Western support of missionary institutions. Many schools, hospitals, and mission stations established by our churches were turned over to the national church when it gained independence. These institutions have become burdens too great for the national churches to bear.

In 1975 I visited an outstanding secondary school that had been built by our church many years ago. It has been and still is the outstanding school of its kind in that country. The director of the school explained that nonfaculty salaries had been increased 50 percent by government action, supplies such as petroleum and food had increased by 50 percent overall, faculty salaries had increased 12 percent. The economic situation in the country made it impossible to increase tuition and other fees and to enroll enough students to keep the school solvent. At that very time the director had received our budget allocation for 1975 and found that we had reduced our giving by one half of the previous year's grant.

The reduction in our grant was based on our own economic situation and priorities. It was made unilaterally. We had not engaged the leadership of this school in dialogue about long-range plans for self-reliance. When we were economically strong we unilaterally contributed large sums of money for capital development and operations. Now that we are in financial difficulty we withdraw in an equally unilateral manner. We are not the only agency that acts this way. Most Western agencies act in the same unilateral manner: the piper calls the tune!

Many responsible leaders in the Third World see dependence opening their churches and institutions not only to domination but in critical moments to possible bankruptcy. This matter of unilateral reductions by donors is a highly sensitive issue. The receiving church rarely has any option but to absorb the blow and suffer the consequences. The damages it is doing to relationships cannot be overstated.

International Economics

The economic problems of 1975 have grown worse in most of the Third World. The economic disease of inflation tends to be far more virulent when communicated to developing countries than it is in the West. The Third World nations simply do not have the economic strength to compete with the West; they are therefore victimized by our inflation.

In the winter of 1974 the Western nations were hit by the shutting off of oil supplies by the Organization of Petroleum Exporting Countries (OPEC). The price we paid to restart the flow of oil created the greatest deficit in United States balance of payments (the difference in cost between what we sell abroad vs. what we buy from other nations) that our nation has ever experienced. It was serious enough to cause some economists to issue dire warnings about the future of our nation's stability. About eighteen months later that crisis had passed and we were again beginning to return to a normal, if not better, balance of payments picture.

Since the price of oil had not declined, and since we were not importing appreciably less oil, how was this miracle accomplished? Economic matters are complicated and no one factor can be credited. However, a very significant factor in the turnaround was the increased price of the products we exported. In raising our prices we not only passed on the additional oil costs but by the very nature of pricing policies, we had added an additional markup for profit. The manufactured goods that we export to Third World nations at these higher prices created added inflation on top of the higher prices which they too were paying for oil. The weak are thus mistreated by the strong.

In the United States our normal response to inflation is to demand higher wages and/or cut back on what we consider unessential cash flow—e.g., our giving to the church or to charitable organizations. In Third World nations the possibility of increasing wages to compensate for inflation has reached a responsible limit. The economy can no longer bear it. Miraculously the giving of most church members overseas does not decline as much as one would expect, but it surely does not increase. The result: the churches are caught in their nations' inflationary spiral. Giving for pastors' salaries and for all other costs goes down or fails to keep pace with inflation. At the same time, Western support is reduced through costs of inflation and/or in real dollars.

Our involvement in the economic crisis of the Third World churches should be apparent. Once again we begin to see that the most guilty person is every one of us.

The economic crisis that is facing most churches around the world is beyond the understanding of most Western Christians. How does one explain the problems created when pensions are not available for pastors who have long since passed retirement age? Or in our Western churches which have an oversupply of trained ministers, how can we communicate the frustration of young people seeking training but finding it economically unattainable? How does one explain the deterioration of church buildings, unpaid teachers in church schools, hospitals unable to buy basic drugs? All these and many other problems rest on the shoulders of Third World church leaders who do not know where to turn for solutions.

From time to time these Third World leaders travel to the West to attend a meeting. They see the way we live, the way our churches are maintained, the unthinking manner of our life-styles. What are their true thoughts? Few ever verbalize their reactions. But a careful study of the literature of moratorium suggests that they have come to the opinion that their churches need to find some way out of dependence on Western churches for support. The growing international eco-

nomic crisis and the role of the Western churches in it
is another factor in the call for a moratorium.

Western Cultural Imperialism

One of the most significant causes of the breakaway
groups, or, in Africa, what we have called the African
independent churches, has been the publishing of the
whole Bible in local languages. Barrett points out that
up until the time the Bible was available in the local
language, the missionaries had had almost absolute control over how the indigenous people understood the
Christian faith. When the Bible was finally published in
their language a momentous change occurred. It then
became possible to differentiate between what the missionaries had said and what the people read for themselves in the Bible.

Barrett says: "In the scriptures, therefore, African
Christians gradually began to detect a basic discrepancy
between missions and scriptures on what were to them
the major points of conflict, namely the traditional customs being attacked by the missions. The slender bibli-
cal basis for monogamy was at once noted. The polyga-
mous practice of the Patriarchs, the vital importance of
family and land, the long lists of respected ancestors,
the Old Testament emphasis upon fertility and sexual-
ity—all these set forth in black and white in the vernac-
ular had a profound impact. Not surprisingly, earnest
Christians came to the same conclusions as did the Ana-
baptist prophets of the Reformation in Europe, namely
that the Old Testament justified polygamy. . . .

"Only one conclusion was possible, for those who
were to become the . . . separatists, concerning this
discrepancy between missions and scriptures: 'The

Watu wa Mungu [People of God] therefore deduced from this fact that the *mzungu,* missionaries, were not interpreting the Bible correctly, and that they only adopted the system of monogamy to suit their own ends.' "46

Other illustrations could readily be cited of what has come to be known as cultural imperialism. Probably the most significant has to do with the use of African instruments, especially the drum, and dancing in worship. Dancing is as much an expression of joy for an African as is a smile. The missionaries' attempts to suppress such an integral and positive part of the culture was based on ignorance and the importation of Western mores.

These and other factors noted earlier point to the need for the Africanization of the Christian faith. In the New Testament, Paul's letters to the churches were attempts to make the early Christian faith, steeped in Jewish culture, relevant to people who were part of Greco-Roman culture. Today, we in the United States have gone beyond Paul's attempts to make the faith relevant to the churches of his day. We have made it relevant to our society in our day. The efforts of earlier missionaries to take their culturally relevant understandings of the faith and impose them on another culture can now be seen as a serious mistake. Thus the present revolt against Western cultural impositions in Third World countries needs to be viewed with the greatest sympathy. We must recognize, however, that it is another factor in the call for a moratorium. All churches, in whatever culture, need to give great attention to the study of the Scriptures and seek the guidance of the Holy Spirit to gain an understanding of where the line must be drawn between the cultural relevance of the Christian faith and culture religion. The two are not the same whether in the Third World or in the United States.

American Superiority and Racism

At the outset it needs to be said that American superiority and racism are not the same. I know of black Americans who have experienced rejection in Africa, not because of racism but because of their American superiority. This suggests that the problem is not an easy one for Americans to sort out. But we may as well start by recognizing that the African can readily distinguish between the two. Furthermore, the African people can distinguish between two types of American superiority.

Racism is a disease of the soul. Whatever its source, it is always evil in its expression. It comes through even when an individual may attempt to hide such an attitude. A racist has no place in the mission of Jesus Christ until the disease of the soul is cured. The tragedy of the history of mission work in Africa is that racists have been attracted to the missionary call and have caused untold damage to the cause of Christ on that continent.

What is called American superiority, however, can be different. Admittedly it is all too often tied up with racism, but not inextricably. The French complain bitterly about American superiority, as do many other white people. The complaint is not uncommon even in Canada.

This nonracist form of superiority can be understood in two ways—and it frequently is by people in Africa. In traveling in Africa I have often been told I am an American by someone who may stop me on the street. The first few times that happened I was so struck by the insight that I inquired as to how my nationality was recognized. Usually the answer was, "By the way you walk." Other mannerisms were sometimes mentioned. To the best of my ability to understand, I have never noted that such persons felt ill at ease because they sense my Americanism. In probing deeper with friends, I have been told that they believe that Americans walk and show other mannerisms which suggest that we know what we are doing and how to go about accomplishing our goals. Those factors, in themselves, are not considered negatively, although they are frequently equated with American superiority.

Another form of superiority comes across as arrogance. Arrogance has been defined as an occupational disease of those who spend their lives directing the intellects of the young. While more negative definitions may be found, that one best serves to explain the problem of many missionaries. The tendency to speak of adults as "dear children," or, even worse, of an adult male employee as "boy," are examples of the problem.

Much more could be said, but an illustration may be more helpful. A Rhodesian friend was talking with me about the matter of race. He told of an experience of going to a white church in Salisbury with a group of fellow students from Epworth Theological College. They had visited this particular church previously; because they sat together they had not caused a commotion. This time one of the seminarians said: "Let's spread out and see what happens." One third of the congregation picked up their Bibles and walked out of church rather than sit next to a black man. It is this nation which today claims it is fighting to preserve Christian civilization!

These, then, are some of the contexts and problems

within which the mission enterprise has been at work. It has helped to form some of the context and created some of the problems. These are factors which are basic to the call for a moratorium.

The Moratorium Policy Stated

The moratorium idea was first discussed in church circles in Asia. It was first voiced here by the Rev. John G. Gatu, General Secretary of the Presbyterian Church of East Africa, in a speech in Milwaukee in October 1971. The matter might have died down had it not been made a central issue at the Assembly of the All-Africa Conference of Churches, held in Lusaka, Zambia, in May 1974.

In the resolution passed by the Lusaka Assembly, there is an introduction which emphasizes the need for African churches to realize their selfhood so they can undertake their part in Christ's mission to the whole world. After calling for a "moratorium on the receiving of money and personnel," it goes on to raise questions about how such a moratorium will affect the churches in Africa and the mission boards in the West. The resolution admits that many present institutional structures in Africa might crumble but adds that a "moratorium on funds and personnel from abroad will, by necessity, enforce the unifying drive of churches in Africa."[47]

Since the Lusaka Assembly, the thrust of that resolution has largely been eroded. As indicated above, few church executives support the idea and almost all churches continue to ask for assistance in the form of personnel and funds. Even the AACC itself, immediately after the Lusaka Assembly, embarked on the building of a headquarters in Nairobi for which a wide appeal was made to Western churches. About the same time, Western churches were requested to supply a missionary to serve the Communications Training Centre of the AACC in Nairobi. That missionary's term has been extended several times and he is still in AACC service.

In a recent conversation with the director of that Centre, the question of the latest extension of service was discussed. The moratorium issue was raised and the question asked as to how an American missionary's presence in the AACC could be justified in the light of the AACC-approved moratorium resolution. His reply was enlightening:

"This man is different. We need him. We have no one available who can do the work he is doing. We are seeking someone to replace him and when we find such a person we need your missionary's service for a year so they can work together. Moratorium is about a different kind of missionary: one who stays on when no longer needed or who attempts to dominate us—that's the kind of missionary to which the call for a moratorium is directed."

Involvement of Congregations at Home

We need to try to understand how the "every one of us" principle is also at work in this matter of moratorium. A man from Africa who was in the United States to obtain a master's degree wrote an article on moratorium for a church paper. I wrote to him to discuss certain statements he had made. In the ensuing correspondence he made the following observation:

"There is no denying of the fact that most white people here are still hung up with false notions of spiritual superiority complexes. As I move about I am tired of being asked such annoying questions as 'How is it over there in our mission field?' or 'How much of your Country is still pagan?' and 'Do your people still resist conversion by our missionaries?' The assumptions behind such questions are obvious."[48]

The tendency on the part of individuals and congregations to elevate "the missionary they know" and our supposed American spiritual status rather than accept the equality of all members of the body of Christ is a serious part of the problem of relationships. It is very much at the heart of the call for a moratorium.

Since this issue was raised at Lusaka, many American denominations have tried in their own way to determine its significance for the future of the mission enterprise. In general the conclusion has been that African delegates may have passed the moratorium resolution at the AACC Assembly but few churches in Africa actually seek such a moratorium.

If one probes deeper, it is possible to determine why the African church representatives in Lusaka passed the resolution and why their leaders who relate to Western churches speak differently. Not long ago the Rev. John Mpaayei said to a group of missionaries in Kenya: "If the churches [African] are to break out of the old environment, and to become truly mature institutions, they must be prepared to take risks and make fundamental changes."[49]

What is the old environment? It is the context of Western superiority, paternalism, and relationships implying racial overtones. The writer of the letter previously quoted speaks to this point in the same letter: "It is true we need partnership, but partnership can only be based on love, equality, and justice. But I suppose the significance of the moratorium in this respect still lies in the fact that the 'younger churches' in the 'Two Thirds' world realize their impotence in a state of continued dependence especially where such dependence is loaded with notions of superiority and inferiority complexes."[50]

The call for a moratorium is a declaration of independence from missionary domination in all forms; it is also a declaration of independence against domination by mission board decisions. The leaders of the churches, who must undertake the burden of keeping inherited programs going, are not able to support the declaration of moratorium for pragmatic reasons. But those who are serious about the mission of the church of Jesus Christ need to give heed. A warning has been sounded. The churches of what we have far too long called the "mission field" have taken their place among us as equals within the universal church of Christ. Our superior attitudes, which have always been sinful, are now intolerable and unacceptable.

QUESTIONS FOR DISCUSSION

1. Does the call for a moratorium suggest that churches in the Third World want isolation from Western churches? If not, what does it suggest?
2. How do you understand the economic problems of the Third World churches? Does their need for our help reflect
    a. Poor management on their part?
    b. Superiority on our part?
    c. A world economic order that favors those who are economically strong?

    d. Their attempt to follow our institutional forms
       of church life?

3. In view of your answer to Question 2, how can Third
   World churches correct the deteriorating situation
   they face? How can we help?

4. What validity do you see in the different denominations we have in America? What validity do you see
   for the different churches within a religious tradition
   such as Lutheran, Reformed, and free? If these differences are valid for peoples of European background, why should African Christians not have freedom also to form church groupings that express their
   understanding of the Christian faith?

5. How do you account for the request for a missionary
   to serve with the AACC Communications Training
   Centre in view of the call for a moratorium? What
   light does it shed on what the African churches are
   trying to tell us?

6

Can the Affluent Sit with the Poor?

Then I came to them . . . and I sat where they sat, and remained there astonished among them seven days. (Ezekiel 3:15, KJV)

There are many reasons why the nineteenth-century missionary movement has come to an end. We have already noted the significant internal factors. There are also political factors. In the first chapter something of the spread of the church was noted. Those who are acquainted with history would understand that the main thrusts of expansion followed the political currents of the day. Paul's missionary journeys were within the Roman Empire of which he was a citizen.

In like manner the nineteenth-century missionary movement was carried on the political currents of the day's colonialism. Following World War I the colonial structures of the world began to deteriorate and after World War II the colonial system virtually collapsed. Nationalism was the new political ideology and the freedom of Western missionaries was sharply curtailed.

Winter points out that 95 percent of the missionary force is serving the area of the 403 million unreached in Africa and Asia mentioned in Chapter 3. Only 5 percent of the Western missionary force is working among the two billion unreached. These 47,500 (the 95 percent) missionaries are working in areas where the church is growing faster than in Western countries.[51] While some of the missionaries are serving national churches, providing skills and experience which the churches do not yet possess, others are part of the problem to which moratorium has been directed. Such a maldistribution of personnel suggests something of the sad state of the present missionary enterprise.

The Worship of Success

Nothing succeeds like success. Right? Wrong! It has not only been policy failures and political changes that have brought to an end the missionary thrust which began in the last century. To a far greater degree than most of us realize, American life-styles based on the affluent society is another major factor.

Since World War II, when America rose to the peak of power in the world, Americans have increasingly identified success with material prosperity. The pursuit of higher standards of living, measured by the things money can buy, has been central to our ambitions. "More is better," our unquestioned philosophy, has fed a growing selfishness in the American spirit.

The worship of success is not a new feature of American life. William James, the American philosopher writing around the turn of the century, called "the exclusive worship of the bitch-goddess SUCCESS" a specifically American "national disease." Today our proclivity to measure success in terms of material possessions is so powerful that it is almost impossible for us to extract ourselves from this way of thinking.

We Americans have become the most affluent nation in the history of mankind. We are less than 6 percent of the world's population but we live off approximately 40 percent of its resources. We are unable to understand what this has done to us as a people. Most of us don't feel rich. Many of us live on the edge of debt; we certainly never seem to have enough income. That is the subtle side of the crisis we face: we *are* the world's most affluent people and yet individually we never seem to have enough.

In recent years, the giving of the membership in American churches to mission has decreased to the point that our ability to work as a partner with churches in other lands has been sharply reduced. This has happened at a time when Western inflation, exported to Third World nations, has created inflation in those nations which is running at a rate of 20 to 30 percent or more. Meanwhile our needs for their raw materials—the main source of jobs and incomes for the Third World peoples—have lessened, reducing the price we pay for these commodities. Our brothers and sisters in the Third World are being ground between the upper and the nether millstone.

At the same time, we are saying to churches whose peoples are economically hurting as we have never hurt that we must now reduce the assistance we give them. They look at us in amazement: the wealthiest nation in the history of the world and not able to help some of the poorest to carry their burdens!

Do we Americans, as a nation, really consider money to be more important than God? The issue was first raised by our Lord as he taught his disciples: "You cannot serve God and Money" (Matt. 6:24, NEB). Obviously the option exists, and as the world's most affluent nation we certainly are prone to the temptation!

The 1976 report of the Overseas Development Council gives us some figures on the distribution of the world's wealth. Gross national product and population figures for 1973 break down as follows:[52]

	GNP %	Population %
North America	30.0	6.1
Europe (excl. U.S.S.R)	31.8	13.2
U.S.S.R.	10.7	6.5
Asia (incl. Middle East; excl. Japan)	10.2	52.7
Japan	8.3	2.8
Central and South America (incl. Mexico)	5.2	7.9
Africa	2.4	10.2
Oceania	1.5	0.6
Total	100.0	100.0

The same report gives some selected examples of how Americans spent their income in 1974, which was $1,406,900,000:[53]

Funeral and burial expenses	$2,700,000
Brokerage charges and investment counseling	2,700,000
Total Overseas Development Assistance	3,300,000
Barbershop, beauty parlor, and bath services	4,200,000

Jewelry and watches	5,800,000
Nondurable toys and sports supplies	8,000,000
Toilet articles and preparations	9,200,000
Cleaning and polishing preparations and miscellaneous household supplies	12,000,000
Radio and television receivers, records, and musical instruments	13,300,000
Tobacco products	13,800,000
Alcoholic beverages	22,900,000

In the 1960's the developed nations, sensing the problem of the world's poverty-stricken countries, committed themselves to an increased development effort for the forthcoming decade. A target of 0.7 percent of the developed nations' GNP was set. The U.S. record is not impressive. In 1960 we gave 0.53 percent of our GNP; by 1970 the figure was 0.31 percent; the 1973 figure of $3,300,000 (noted above) is 0.30 percent. The record of the richest nation on earth is that it gives to help alleviate the world's need, just a bit more than it spends on servicing its private investments!

The preliminary estimate of our giving for overseas development for 1977 is 0.17 percent. To understand how serious has been our movement toward serving our own life-styles, this 1977 figure should be compared with our record of giving in 1947, at the time of the Marshall Plan, 2.79 percent.[54]

In view of this record of growing self-centeredness, is it any wonder that James Reston, writing in *The New York Times,* quotes a Latin-American leader as saying: "I would like to say that in reality there is a Latin-American blockade on the United States. It is a blockade in the minds of the peasants, the workers, the university students, and the new generation. It is a psychological blockade, a moral blockade that the United States is not going to erode until it radically changes its policy *vis-à-vis* Latin America."[55]

The *Manchester Guardian* of April 29, 1971, records this warning: "Failure to give sufficient aid to developing countries would have to be measured 'in terms of sickness, hunger, decay and perhaps bloodshed,' Lord Greenwood, the former Labour Minister, told the Lords yesterday in a debate on foreign aid. 'If we do not discharge our moral responsibility, if the hungry third world resorts increasingly to violence and political extremism—at least some of the blame will rest on our shoulders.' " And since then, our giving has decreased —and world unrest has increased as predicted.

This secular state of world affairs is reflected in our church giving to assist Third World churches. By our failure we are destroying our witness to the fact that in Christ, God has penetrated the evil of this world and brought good news.

This self-serving concentration on higher standards of living for ourselves we call "success."

Who Will Go?

We still have a mandate . . . Who will go? The command of our Lord to be his witnesses has not been abrogated by the failures of the missionary enterprise, the political situation, or American materialism. The manner in which we are able to carry out a witness for Christ is different today from what it was 150 years ago. But the need for trained, committed persons is as great as ever.

To be the carriers of good news today, persons must

first of all have a clear knowledge of their relationship to Jesus Christ. But in most countries of the world, such persons must also have the kind of training and/or experience that will permit them to train others in some form of basic skills. Technical skills, skills in food production which includes water resources as well as agricultural skills, health care, and in a few places the teaching of secondary school subjects—all these are in demand: The churches of the Third World are calling for help in their witness and service to their people.

Are affluent Americans prepared to respond to these needs? On the whole the answer seems to be "no." The experience of most mission agencies in recruiting doctors has been bleak. Academic teachers are available, but people who can teach technical subjects are almost impossible to recruit for overseas service—for example, well drillers or agriculturalists. Some illustrations of the problem may help to explain our difficulty.

We Americans assume certain conditions as being "basic" to life. Suppose a person capable of teaching in a theological school (a need of some churches) were to accept a call to serve in country A. The school where the person would teach is located far from a main city. The housing for faculty members is old and lacks electricity and running water. What does one do? Call on the church at home to provide funds to rehabilitate the house in which the American will live? Or should the funds be requested to rehabilitate the houses of all the teachers at this school? (Would there be a response to such a request?) Or does one simply try to get along without the things that at home are considered to be necessities? If so, will the family be able "to take it" for the sake of the work that is being done?

Suppose that same family, going to that situation, has

school-age children. If they are in any of the grades from 1 to 8, they can live in the capital city, some four to five hours' drive away: If they are in high school, they must travel to a neighboring country and will be able to come home only two or three times a year. Or, there is another option. They may go to a national school and study in a foreign language in a curriculum that is not oriented toward entrance into an American university. In the context of American society today, are there many families willing to make these sacrifices?

Let us change the person and the assignment. An American surgeon accepts a call to serve in a church hospital in country Y. The housing may be better than that described in country A, but the hospital is most unsatisfactory. The X-ray equipment has to be repaired frequently and the surgeon must make the repairs: Parts are hard to come by. The operating theater lacks many of the normally accepted necessities. The pharmacy is stocked only with basic drugs, and some of them are in short supply. There is no anesthesiologist, so with the help of a national nurse the surgeon must oversee that job personally. The capital city is three hours' drive away. The hospital has only one car which has seen extensive service and is not too dependable. The educational possibilities for the children are similar to those in country A.

Again, what does the American surgeon do? Call on the church at home to put on a fund drive to get better equipment for the hospital and to get the family a private car? If so, what does this say to the other members of the hospital staff?

These are not unrealistic situations dreamed up to make a point. Each of them is a real place with a genuine need for persons to serve in order that the local

church may carry on its witness for Christ. They illustrate two problems: (1) the problem related to the giving of financial help; and (2) the problem of finding
persons capable and willing to serve in places of need
around the world.

The idea that we can do what we used to do—go into
an area, build a mission compound in which Americans
can live with a degree of comfort, and maintain that
compound through our financial resources—is simply
no longer valid.

On the other hand, while there are many young persons who are willing to accept service abroad under
difficult conditions, most of them do not have the experience required to meet the needs. Most churches have
a supply of college graduates from which to draw. The
needs of these churches lie in the area of persons with
postgraduate training and experience in the subjects
mentioned above. But persons with such training have
"a stake" in the American way of life. Adjustment to
service abroad is difficult. We have become unconscious
captives of our American affluence.

And finally, only the poor in spirit need apply. There
is no place for superiority, economic or cultural. Above
all, those who are willing to accept these service oppor-
tunities must know the living presence of Christ in a
way that can be communicated by both word and deed.

The Burial Ground of Moral Integrity

We are discussing realistic obstacles to the renewal of
the Christian mission as we look forward to that
renewal. In the early days of the nineteenth-century
missionary movement the church was involved in the
social affairs of its day. The same awakening in the

church which launched the missionary movement also launched social crusades in areas of prison reform, child labor, the abolition of the slave trade, and other reforms. The gospel speaks to the wholeness of all peoples.

There were many even then who opposed such social reforms. Slavery was a lucrative trade from which Britain profited greatly. Yet, in the end, the church of Jesus Christ responding to the demands of the gospel won the day. And if there is to be a renewal of mission today, we must face the same sort of issues.

Speaking to the Fifth Assembly of the World Council of Churches, Prime Minister Michael N. Manley of Jamaica said: "If capitalism was the engine that lifted man to new levels of economic and technological progress, it was equally the burial ground of his moral integrity."

Mr. Manley is no friend of capitalism but he is a Christian and a highly respected leader of his church. Why has he taken such a jaundiced view of our American economic philosophy?

The Christian Science Monitor of October 23, 1975, reports on an address delivered by the United States ambassador to the United Nations, Daniel P. Moynihan, to the Business Council, an organization of one hundred of the nation's top corporation executives. Ambassador Moynihan said that they should be concerned about the future of democracy and free enterprise because there are only "about two dozen democracies and two dozen free-enterprise countries remaining in the world." He added, "Democracies are becoming a recessive form of government, like monarchies used to be—something the world is moving from, rather than to." Why are we in trouble?

The answer to these questions was suggested in a speech to the Purdue National Meeting of the United Presbyterian Women in July 1976 by Ronald E. Müller, a social scientist. Dr. Müller is co-author of *Global Reach*, a volume on transnational corporations, and a frequent consultant in corporate board rooms. In his speech Dr. Müller makes two salient points. His first is a summary of much that is covered above: "There are more hungry people today than at any other time in the past thirty years: more people both in an absolute sense and more people as a percentage of the world's population."[56]

His other point is that in the past thirty years "we have witnessed one revolution after another in a series of technological, communication, and organizational breakthroughs."[57] These changes have taken us from a "nationally integrated society into the age of a globally interdependent nation in terms of our economics and politics, but still lacking a global consciousness."[58]

He supports this statement with impressive illustrations and documentation. If this is true, our natural tendency to think in terms of what is good for our country becomes a danger to the well-being of all people on earth. In this context, an affluent America living unto itself and maximizing its profits from trade with other nations is no different in the world context from white South Africans maximizing their income from the labor of blacks in their country.

In illustrating some of the ways in which multinational corporations maximize profits at the expense of poor nations, Müller argues that the individual responsible is also a victim of the system. He asked the director of an overseas subsidiary, "Aren't you feeling bad about this?" The director responded: "What can I do? First of all, if I weren't willing to do this, I'd be replaced by someone else from within the company who's trying to get this position. And second of all, if my company did not do this, but all the other companies continued to do it, where would we be vis-à-vis our stockholders and our profits, three or four or five years from now?"[59]

Müller later points out, "The result is a systemic dilemma, characterized by concentrated power and a kind of strange nonmarket competition that no longer assures accountability."[60]

Müller calls for the church to take up a crusade for the resurrection of human values. The point is well made. In reaching toward ever more affluent life-styles we have lost our moral integrity. We have forgotten that our affluence, in a globally interconnected world, is another man's hunger. Mission and justice cannot be separated.

Where Is the Mission Field?

For you say, I am rich, I have prospered, and I need nothing; not knowing that you are wretched, pitiable, poor, blind, and naked. (Rev. 3:17)

The growth of the church in many countries of the Third World is accompanied by a revolution against missionary control. This clearly suggests the insensitivity of speaking of "our mission fields" as being "over there." Where, then, are the mission fields today?

The meeting in Mexico of the Commission on World Mission and Evangelism of the World Council of Churches first raised the issue of seeing mission as a six-continent challenge. The point is well taken. The recent history of the church in Europe has been one of ebb. In North America there has been a sharp decline in church membership since the 1950's. Both continents suffer from the materialism which erodes the very essence of the Christian faith.

In this context, my own denomination, the United Presbyterian Church, has been attempting to organize a ministry to America by church leaders from the Third World. Several years ago a bishop of the Church of North India, the Right Reverend Ramchandra S. Bhandare, served in the northwestern part of the United States in such a capacity. His report illustrates our condition of feeling that we have need of nothing which I daresay is typical of the main-line denominations generally:

"I tried to explain to the congregations that the 'Mission of the Church is *Christ's* mission to the world' and we, as Christians from all over the world, are called to participate in *His* service. He provides the necessary power and guidance. He invites us to forget ourselves, our petty self-centeredness and craving for recognition and share with him the burden of concern for the whole world. *The terms 'Mission in the Ecumenical Era,' or the 'Internationalization of the Mission,' or the 'Ecumenical Sharing of Personnel' are neither understood nor appreciated by most of the members of the congregations (in the United States). It is news to them that the churches of Asia could send missionaries to the other parts of the world.* The idea of having a missionary from 'the Third World' is new and strange to many. I was advised personally not to speak about ecumenical mission. . . . One day I asked a small group of women whether they would like to have an Indian woman, a qualified and committed Christian, to work among them as a missionary. Neither did they expect this question nor could they answer it. But in reply they raised a question, *'But what will she do?'* As the modern missionary movement began from Europe and North America, many members of the congregations still believe that *only they can send missionaries abroad."*

It is unimportant that American congregations do not know all the terms of the professional jargon about mission today. What is extremely important is the general impression given to Bishop Bhandare that we American Christians have need of nothing. "But what will she do?" expresses well our feeling of spiritual contentment. Could it be that God is saying to us American Christians that we are "wretched, pitiable, poor, blind, and naked"?

Bishop Bhandare was impressed with the "busyness" of American life. In an aside he writes: "Many of us who come from the Third World are not yet prepared to move with the same speed as you are accustomed to here. . . . From the day of my arrival in Seattle until I completed the ninety days, I was kept busy. I thought 'slave drivers' died a natural death with the end of the slave trade, but this may be a new trade, with business-like drivers."

But his concern was not only for himself; it was for the spiritual life of American Christians. In another part of his report he writes: "I was hoping to know the life and work of the pastors from close quarters. But only a few of them could find it convenient to give their time to me. They seemed to be always very busy doing things. I wonder whether they find some time in the morning, before the telephones start ringing, for quiet meditation and prayer."

It is common for people from the Third World to comment about the hurried activity which we call life in the United States. Is it possible that much of this activity is an attempt to escape from the reality of our condition? Bishop Bhandare complimented American churches for their concern for "Global Mission," but then went on to say: *"However, to many Christians in the U.S.A. the 'Global Mission' does not include the U.S.A.* Some elderly persons have shared with me their deep concern *for the high percentage of crimes and divorces, the existing immorality, the young addicts to drugs and liquor, etc. Whenever I invited attentions of the congregations in my sermons to see the afflictions and hear the cries of their own young people, many have not appreciated it.* Did not Jesus Christ ask His disciples to witness unto Him in Jerusalem, Judea, Samaria and to the uttermost part of the world?"

On the matter of the use of our money, Bishop Bhandare also has some insights: "The giving of the members toward the support of the work of the church, including worldwide mission, I am told is improving. But when we consider the percentage in relation to family income there is great room for improvement. Church members should give 10 percent, not 2 1/2 or 4 percent.

"Secondly, I regret to say that many of the congregations are not fully committed to the mission work, outside their church. . . . In a church I visited, even after seeing slides of Christians without a roof over their heads, a member showed me the plan of a new and modern kitchen they are about to build. *It clearly indicates local church needs have first priority. We talk about 'commitment' but we live as uncommitted Christians.* We talk about and celebrate the sacrifice of Jesus

Christ, but we are not prepared to live a sacrificial life. Most of us are participating in Christ's mission, with whatever is left over.

"Three or four times in my sermons I referred to a part of the WCC report which reads, 'Three quarters of the world's income, investments, sciences, and 90 percent of world resources are in the hands of one quarter of its people.'. . . I could see the restlessness of some Christians in their pews. . . . One of the pastors asked me, 'Bishop, are you jealous and angry with us after seeing all that we have and how we use it?' *My answer to him was, 'No, but both the poor nations and the rich nations are equally in need of deliverance and God's guidance.'*"

The question of whether the affluent can sit with the poor is a basic question for the American church today. The future of mission, the very future of the church in America, may well depend on how well we respond to God's call to repentance.

> Those whom I love, I reprove and chasten; so be zealous and repent. (Rev. 3:19)

QUESTIONS FOR DISCUSSION

1. In the light of the "2 billion unreached," why do you suppose so many missionaries are at work in areas where the church is dynamic and growing? What do these statistics have to say to the calls for more evangelists to reach people in the areas where the church is strong?

2. The picture of American wealth and how we use it is distressing—and frustrating. What can you as an

individual do about it? What hope do you see that our affluent life-style can be altered and reverse our present trend toward increasing self-centeredness?

3. Discuss the problems that face an American missionary described in this chapter. Are there qualified people whom you know who could serve under these conditions? Are they willing to go? If they did go and wrote home about the physical problems under which they live and work, would you send money to help them? If you did, what recommendation would you make about how the money should be used?

4. We Americans consider our standard of living to be the result of our hard work. What is your reaction to Müller's argument that we live in a globally interconnected nation? What connection do you see between our prosperity and the poverty of other nations? What is your reaction to OPEC's raising the price of crude oil? or coffee-producing nations' raising the price of coffee beans? Do you feel the same way when we raise the price of our manufactured products? But is it fair for Arab oil sheiks to get richer at the expense of the poor? Is it fair for Americans to get richer at the expense of the poor?

5. Does Bishop Bhandare's report upset you? If so, are you disturbed because what he says is wrong or because it attacks our American life-style? Why is it important for such questions to be raised for discussion in our churches? What relationship do you see between these issues and Moynihan's remarks about the decline of democracies? What choices is God placing before us?

7

The Renewal of the Christian Mission

The Spirit of the Lord is upon me,
because he has anointed me to preach
    good news to the poor.
He has sent me to proclaim release
    to the captives
and recovering of sight to the blind,
to set at liberty those who are oppressed,
to proclaim the acceptable year of the Lord.

(Luke 4:18-19)

Today the message that our Lord came to proclaim is more relevant than ever before. The poor cry out for good news. Prisoners of oppression await release. Those who are blinded by ideologies of right and left need recovery of sight. The broken victims of this world's struggles long to be freed.

The gospel is the proclamation that in Jesus Christ, God has triumphed over all the powers of sin and evil. The resurrection of Christ is God's sign that God has intervened in the life of the world and brought the new creation into being. It was the proclamation of Christ's resurrection that gave the early Christians the assurance of God's triumph. They did not fear death, because in Christ God had destroyed death and all the powers of evil. That faith resulted not only in the founding of the church but also in its expansion throughout the world.

The church in America has many resources to bring to the service of the worldwide church. In a time when faith is in crisis, we need to understand both our strengths and our problems.

Adolf Harnack, the historian of the early centuries of the church, writes: "Tertullian cries to the authorities: 'The oftener we are mown down by you, the larger grow our numbers. The blood of Christians is a seed. . . . That very obstinacy which you reprobate is our instructress.' The most numerous and successful missionaries of the Christian religion were not the regular teachers but Christians themselves by dint of their loyalty and courage. . . .

"It was characteristic of their religion that everyone who seriously confessed the faith proved of service to its propaganda. Christians are to 'let their light shine, that pagans may see their good works and glorify the Father in heaven.' If this dominated all their life, and if they lived according to the precepts of their religion, they could not be hidden at all; by their very mode of living they could not fail to preach their faith plainly and audibly. . . .

"We cannot hesitate to believe that the great mission of Christianity was in reality accomplished by means of informal missionaries. Justin says so quite explicitly. What won him over was the impression made by the moral life which he found among Christians in general. How this life stood apart from that of pagans even in the ordinary round of the day, how it had to be or ought to be a constant declaration of the gospel—all this is vividly portrayed by Tertullian."[61]

The Crisis of Faith

The great problem of the church in America is that we have fallen victim to the tyranny of our age. We wrestle with an established form of Christianity. Many of us who are called "Christian" bear that name because it is something that came down to us from our parents, and probably their parents before them. The power of Christ's life-changing presence is missing. The temptation to find fulfillment in America's affluence is overwhelming. Far too many have surrendered to materialism. Like the Israelites in Canaan, we are trying to serve both the Lord of Hosts and the Baalim (materialism) of the people among whom we dwell. Our Lord's warning that we cannot serve two masters is made evident by the spiritual anemia of most Christians.

For most of us, our crisis is that we are blind to our problem. Like Israel of old, we listen readily to those who tell us soothing words and try to destroy the prophets sent by God. But because we are called by Christ's name, God will not let us alone, but calls us to repent, leave our worship of false gods, and return to him.

The "American Dream" has already suffered from Vietnam, the youth revolution, Watergate, and the OPEC oil embargo. The cold winter of 1976–77 allows us a glimpse of how fragile our affluent society can be before the forces of nature. Whether we have recognized it or not, we are being tested by God. The question is how we are going to respond.

W. A. Visser 't Hooft, former General Secretary of the

World Council of Churches, has said: "The faith that is
tested produces hope. It is one of the strangest aspects
of the history of the Church that the churches under
pressure often know so much more about hope than the
untroubled churches. There is the joy of experiencing
that, in spite of the difficulty of the examination of one's
obvious incapacity to respond adequately, one is some-
how allowed to pass. There is the joy that, in spite of all
the closing of doors, the Word of God still finds holes
through which it can creep. And here is above all the
glad discovery that we are taken up in the great hap-
penedness which goes on happening and will lead to
the ultimate event of the manifest victory of Christ.

"If it is at the point of its missionary witness that the
Church is specially tested, it is also at that point that it
is given ground for hope."[62]

This crisis, or testing of faith, through which we are
now passing can give us depression, or it can produce
hope. If we have given ourselves over to the affluent
society, to the materialism of our day, then our day-by-
day decisions are ruled by our commitment to those
gods. The time of testing now upon us will be depress-
ing indeed. But if our faith is in God, who caused our
Lord Jesus Christ to rise from the dead, then for us even
death itself is truly swallowed up in victory. We can face
whatever must come in confidence because our day-to-
day decisions are made in the context of our faith in
Christ.

The Christian Community and Mission

Once we Americans can be relieved of concerns
about our future, and God's Holy Spirit moves in our
congregations in renewal, there will be a new sense of

our calling to be God's witnesses. Many of the problems that now beset our mission efforts will begin to be resolved.

Throughout this book we have been seeing that the most guilty person is every one of us. Our proclivity to blame the problems of the present decline in mission on others is counterproductive. We have seen some of the problems that missionaries have helped to create, but we have also seen that missionaries only reflect the fellowship from which they come. The boards and agencies of our denominations have also created problems, but they are servants of their denominations and reflect their congregations' outlook. There are tensions within that triangle—congregation, missionary, and mission agency—part is a healthy tension but another part grows out of issues already raised.

No one should or can say how all the negative tensions should be resolved. But it may prove helpful to open some windows based on the insights gathered in earlier chapters.

The Congregation and Mission

We can start with a clear affirmation: Christ's followers have not and never will be relieved of the responsibility of witnessing and carrying on mission in his name. Ogbu U. Kalu, a lecturer in the Department of Religion, University of Nigeria, Nsukka, has written: "Each member of Christ's body is called and each is sent. The scriptures are full of condemnations of the apathetic servants who do not obey their master's call, who are unfruitful and who do not use their talent."[63]

Each church in every nation is first of all called to be effective in witness to its neighbors and its society. Because God's church is alive throughout the world, we can no longer afford to be so concerned about the "heathen over there" as to have no time for those about us. Only as we fulfill our Lord's commandment to be his witnesses in our own vicinity are we prepared to move on to "Samaria and to the end of the earth." All too many Christians have given their money to mission because they feel guilty about their own personal witness and life-style. That is not the path of renewal.

Another important window that needs to be opened in the congregations of America is a willingness to hear what Christians from other lands have to say to us. The response, in the previous chapter, to Bishop Bhandare —"What will she do?"—is an indication of our self-centeredness. In this connection, the late D. T. Niles, General Secretary of the East Asia Christian Conference, has said: "In fact, the necessity of the foreign missionary is a universal necessity. 'Because we have come to terms with our own society,' says Dr. Matthews, 'the total Word of God has to be declared to us by another.' "[64]

This understanding of the foreign missionary has been given permanent and universal importance by our Lord's command, "teaching them to observe all that I have commanded you" (Matt. 28:20). No people, no culture, has total insight, nor is it totally faithful to all that our Lord has commanded us. We need one another.

If the congregations in the American church will pursue every opportunity to hear what church leaders from other lands and cultures have to say to us, our preoccupation and misconceptions about the place of the missionary in God's total plan for mission will largely dissolve.

The Missionary and Mission

There is a place for Americans in mission abroad. But that place has clearly changed, and will continue to change. Our paternalistic emphasis in the sending of "evangelists to the heathen" has been judged in the light of church growth in other countries and our own spiritual decline in America.

A large part of our problem lies in our concept of evangelism. For too long, evangelism has meant telling spirits with ears the way of salvation. There seems to have been no willingness to accept the wholeness of the human being. The other side of that false coin is equally invalid: that to improve a person's social condition is all that is necessary to salvation. No society, no ideology, has proved adequate to wash away the "fallout from Adam" which erodes the best of human intentions. Evangelism is the need for so communicating the gospel in its wholeness that Christ's life, death, and resurrection may transform both persons *and the society that people create.*

To that end Americans filled with the love of Jesus Christ and able to communicate their love for and knowledge of Christ are needed. While that requirement is basic, it is not enough. We Americans are technically trained and the skills that we have are in great demand in the Third World. It is not good enough to send our unskilled—the Third World churches have those in abundance. They need our skilled persons. They need the persons who could be successful in our society—doctors, nurses, agriculturalists. They also need persons who know how to drill for water, and gifted trades persons who can teach carpentry, masonry, mechanics, and all the other trades necessary to make an economy function.

Those who go must be willing to identify with the people among whom they work. Identification is no mechanical thing. It is not living exactly as others live, nor does it mean speaking their language fluently. It does not even mean living within their income. Primarily, identification is a spiritual relationship, and if it is present, all of the above will always be held in tension with it. Then we will never allow our differences, whatever they are, to become an offense. When we identify, we will feel the hurts that come in the lives of others through repressive governments, poverty, inadequate health care, and so many of the other factors that dominate the peoples of the Third World.

Identification brings understanding—understanding of the failures in others, which so often are different from our failings and thus are harder for us to excuse. But if there is true identification, we not only understand one another's failings but begin to find ways in which to explore them together in the light of Scripture.

Finally, identification will mean that missionaries gain understanding of the reasons behind wealth in one country and poverty in another. That knowledge will become so important that they will find ways to communicate it to those to whom they speak, because they see the source of the problem in a new way.

The Mission Agency and Mission

A careful reading of the statements on moratorium coming from the Third World leadership will suggest that the main thrust is against the structures of mission even more than against the missionary. Carr's statement that mission agencies are "perpetrators of structural violence . . . and they should be abolished" is probably the strongest statement on record. The AACC call for a moratorium says, "Should the moratorium cause missionary sending agencies to crumble, the African Church would have performed a service in redeeming God's people in the northern hemisphere from a distorted view of the mission of the Church in the world."[65]

What, then, is the future of the mission agencies? Clearly there is need for a radical review of the need for these agencies in their historic sense. We have already noted how the power formerly dispersed has flowed back to the agencies at home. The related churches around the world are no longer willing to be subjected to foreign domination, whether through a foreign mission in their land or from some agency in America.

Some denominations have begun to move away from positions of domination. Others have made cosmetic changes which are not satisfactory to related churches. Few if any have gone far enough.

The problem is that consciously or unconsciously we still think in terms of oversight. As foreign missions began to integrate into national churches, the boards at home expanded their staffs. Why? Obviously to give the oversight which the now defunct foreign missions previously supplied. Today we are still trying to solve the problems of a new epoch while relying on the assumptions and methods of a moribund one. We still expend too much money and energy maintaining structures to serve the past at precisely a time when related churches do not seek our guidance or trust our expertise, and are not willing to put up with our oversight.

But the bureaucracies of our denominations are created by and for the congregations that they serve. Only as the renewal of the total church in mission becomes a reality will our structures of mission change.

The churches of the Third World seek relationships of equality. The church in Korea, or Kenya, or Brazil wants to be treated in the same way as the church in Great Britain. There is no room any longer for two levels of relationship. Our ways of attempting to solve problems in the past will work no longer. The support staffs in mission agencies which seek to facilitate the living and work of missionaries only tie those missionaries to our church psychologically, and are therefore counterproductive.

The so-called business methods, imposed by those who feel that the bureaucracies can be made more efficient if run in a businesslike way, only accentuate the irrelevancy of our outdated agencies. Such methods may create demands relevant to an affluent American business style, but they increase the aggravation of related churches that cannot afford our computer-age management methods.

Just as so many persons in the American congregations have hung on to the concepts of the nineteenth-century missionary movement, so the church and its agencies have hung on to the idea that the continuation of the agency bureaucracies is important to mission. The death of the nineteenth-century missionary structures will not be the death of the Christian mission. Rather, the death of the old system is essential for the coming of a new day of mutual service of all the churches that comprise Christ's body.

The Body of Christ and Mission

The renewal of the Christian mission is as radical as returning to the concept that Paul sets forth in his first letter to the Corinthians: "For just as the body is one and has many members, and all the members of the body, though many, are one body, so it is with Christ. . . . God has so adjusted the body . . . that the members may have the same care for one another. If one member suffers, all suffer together; if one member is honored, all rejoice together. Now you are the body of Christ and individually members of it" (I Cor. 12:12,24–27).

We are living in a day when Christ's body consists of his people in every continent on earth. The fact that we are one third of the earth's people clearly calls us to be effective witnesses to the other two thirds of our global neighbors. Our disunited, Western-dominated approach to the three great communities of peoples who have resisted Christ's gospel thus far should be seen as God's call to renewal and unity. We *are* one body. Efforts toward organic unity are less important than the spirit we show in working in the midst of our present structural and national divisions.

The spirit in which we approach each of the issues raised in this book is crucial to renewal. None of us can achieve the resolution of all the problems that affect us. They are too great, too all-encompassing, to respond to individual efforts. But in the power of the Holy Spirit each of us can make a beginning: in the next decision we make, in the next discussion we have, in the next opportunity we have to influence a group decision.

If with all our being we are seeking the renewal of our faith and the Christian mission, God, through the renewing presence of the Holy Spirit, will give us power to be a part of that mission wherever we may be. Yes, the renewal of the Christian mission is a call for a radical change in our lives. It is a call radical enough to show that we truly love one another whatever our race or nation.

Kalu puts all of this in these words: "The moratorium call is even more radical than those who have reacted so defensively to it realize. It is no less than a call, not to new forms, but to a new Covenant, not to new relationships but to a renewed Body."[66]

Notes

1. *Moratorium, A Strategy of Self-Reliance* (Nairobi: All-Africa Conference of Churches, 1975).

2. Jose Miguez-Bonino, "The Present Crisis in Mission," *The Church Herald*, Nov. 12, 1971.

3. Burgess Carr, "Internationalizing the Mission," in Joel Underwood (ed.), *In Search of Mission: An Interconfessional and Intercultural Quest*, The Future of the Missionary Enterprise Series: Dossier 9 (IDOC, 1974), p. 74.

4. The quotations from African church leaders here and in the preceding paragraph are from notes of personal conversations.

5. Thomas Leeuw, in Underwood (ed.), *In Search of Mission*, p. 66.

6. Tertullian, Apol. L (translation from *The Oxford Dictionary of Quotations*).

7. Kenneth Scott Latourette, *A History of Christianity* (Harper & Brothers, 1953), p. 90.

8. *Ibid.*, pp. 269–270.

9. *Ibid.*, p. 385.

10. *Ibid.*, p. 1003.

11. *Ibid.*, p. 968.

12. J. Wesley Bready, *This Freedom—Whence?* (American Tract Society, 1942), p. 65.

13. *Ibid.*, p. 86.

14. John Wesley, *Wesley His Own Biographer* (London: C. H. Kelly, 1891), p. 70.

15. Latourette, *A History of Christianity*, p. 1026.

16. Arthur E. R. Boak, Albert Hyma, and P. W. Slosson, *The Growth of European Civilization* (F. S. Crofts & Co., Inc., 1938), p. 213. Bready, *op. cit.*, makes this same point in his chapter "The Emergence of a Prophet."

17. Latourette, *A History of Christianity*, p. 1019.

18. Kenneth Scott Latourette, *A History of the Expansion of Christianity*, Vol. VII, *Advance Through Storm: A.D. 1914 and After, with Concluding Generalizations* (Harper & Brothers, 1945), p. 465.

19. J. Herbert Kane, *Two-Fold Growth* (China Inland Mission, 1947), p. 41.

20. Arthur F. Glasser, "The 'New' Overseas Missionary Fellowship," unpublished paper, Philadelphia, Oct. 1, 1965.

21. Carr, in Underwood (ed.), *In Search of Mission*, p. 73.

22. Roland Allen, *Missionary Methods: St. Paul's or Ours?* (Wm. B. Eerdmans Publishing Company, 1962), pp. 143ff.

23. Latourette, *Advance Through Storm*, p. 50.

24. Allen, *op. cit.*, p. 144.

25. Latourette, *Advance Through Storm*, pp. 462, 464.

26. *Ibid.*, p. 463.

27. Ralph D. Winter, *The World Christian Movement 1950–1975: An Interpretive Essay*, pamphlet (William Carey Library, 1975), p. 6.

28. David B. Barrett, "A.D. 2000: 350 Million Christians in Africa," *International Review of Missions*, January 1970, p. 49.

29. Gidada Solon, *The Other Side of Darkness* (Friendship Press, 1972), p. 28.

30. Stanton R. Wilson, "Report of the Representative in Korea, 1975, Silence–Systems–Self-Development—Salvation," p. 10. Unpublished paper.

31. *Ibid.*

32. David B. Barrett, *Schism and Renewal in Africa: An Analysis of Six Thousand Contemporary Religious Movements* (Nairobi: Oxford University Press, 1968), p. 6.

33. *Ibid.*, p. 167.

34. The Lausanne Covenant. Lausanne '74—International Congress on World Evangelization, Lausanne, Switzerland, July 16–25, 1974. Persons attended from 150 countries.

35. Ralph D. Winter, "Seeing the Task Graphically," *Evan-*

gelical Missions Quarterly, January 1974. Reprinted as a pamphlet by William Carey Library, p. 15.

36. *Ibid.,* p. 6.

37. Martin Luther King, Jr., a letter written in response to a statement made by eight clergymen (including a rabbi, one Episcopal bishop, one Roman Catholic bishop, and two United Methodist bishops) calling the Birmingham demonstrations "unwise and untimely," from *Christianity and Crisis,* May 27, 1963.

38. John Bright, quoted by Tom Mboya, *Conflict and Nationhood* (London: The Africa Bureau, 1963), p. 5.

39. Julius Nyerere, "Under Racism, Man Either Becomes Less than a Man, or He Must Fight," *Justice,* February/March 1971, p. 26.

40. Orlando E. Costas, "Mission Out of Affluence," *Missiology,* October 1973, p. 410.

41. David M. Paton, *Christian Missions and the Judgment of God* (London: SCM Press, Ltd, 1953), pp. 43–46.

42. David J. Bosch, *The Church in South Africa—Tomorrow,* printed as a supplement to *Ecunews,* the news service of the South Africa Council of Churches, 1975, pp. 4–5.

43. Desmond Tutu, a private letter to Prime Minister John Vorster, printed in *Ecunews,* May 26, 1976, after the prime minister's reply was received.

44. Burgess Carr, "The Engagement of Lusaka," in *The Struggle Continues, Lusaka 1974* (Nairobi: All-Africa Conference of Churches, 1975), p. 77.

45. Ecumenical Sharing of Personnel, Interim Committee Report, Choully, July 1972, Appendix IIIB.

46. Barrett, *Schism and Renewal in Africa,* p. 128.

47. Mandates from Lusaka, "The Call for a Moratorium," Report of Work Group 3, *The Struggle Continues, Lusaka 1974,* p. 53.

48. Letter from Nyansako-ni-Nku to Paul A. Hopkins, January 18, 1976.

49. Quoted in a speech by Rev. John G. Gatu to the Church Missionary Society (Anglican) Conference, Limuru, Kenya, April 10, 1973.

50. Letter from Nyansako-ni-Nku.

51. Ralph D. Winter, *Seeing the Task Graphically,* p. 8.

52. *The U.S. and World Development: Agenda for Action, 1976,* prepared by Roger D. Hansen and the staff of the Overseas Development Council (Praeger Publishers, 1976), p. 129.

53. *Ibid.,* p. 208.

54. *Ibid.,* p. 203.

55. Luis Echeverría Álvarez, quoted by James Reston in *The New York Times,* Aug. 27, 1975.

56. Ronald E. Müller, "Reactivating Human Values in a Transformed World," speech to Purdue 1976 National Meeting of United Presbyterian Women, *Concern,* November 1976, p. 29.

57. *Ibid.,* p. 30.

58. *Ibid.,* p. 31.

59. *Ibid.,* p. 32.

60. *Ibid.,* p. 33.

61. Adolf Harnack, *The Expansion of Christianity in the First Three Centuries* (G. P. Putnam's Sons, 1904), Vol. I, pp. 458–460.

62. W. A. Visser 't Hooft, "Missions as the Test of Faith," a paper presented to the Commission on World Mission and Evangelism, World Council of Churches, Mexico City, 1963, p. 6.

63. Ogbu U. Kalu, "Not Just New Relationships but a Renewed Body," *International Review of Missions,* April 1975, p. 144.

64. D. T. Niles, "A Church and Its Selfhood," an unpublished paper, p. 15.

65. "The Call for a Moratorium," *The Struggle Continues, Lusaka 1974,* p. 53.

66. Kalu, *loc. cit.,* p. 147.